BONNY'S AMERICA

CUT THE WOMAN SOME SLACKS!

BONNY'S AMERICA

CUT THE WOMAN SOME SLACKS!

Bonny Belgum

K e n A r n o l d B o o k s LLC
Portland, Oregon

Publisher's Note: All names and identifying characteristics have been
changed to protect the privacy of the individuals involved.

Some of the essays in this book appeared previously—sometimes
under different titles and/or in earlier versions—in the following
publications: *Minneapolis Star Tribune, Atlanta Journal-Constitution,
St. Paul Pioneer Press,* and *The Minnesota Women's Press.*

Library of Congress Control Number: 2008927446

Published by KenArnoldBooks, LLC,
1330 SW 3rd Avenue, 810, Portland, OR 97201

ISBN: 978-0-9799634-7-6

www.kenarnoldbooks.com

for my husband Erik,
the answer to prayers I didn't dare to pray,
dreams I didn't dare to dream

CONTENTS

1. If My Pay's Low, I Must Be Belgum

I Wouldn't Swear to the Accuracy of These Statements

I once enjoyed a career as a typo-chaser for a personal injury law firm.

In this capacity, I observed that those around me who work too hard tend to lose perspective and the hilarity that it generally brings. The following entertainment is presented to you courtesy of legal secretaries' typos and automatic-pilot spellchecking (okay, mostly mine), lawyers' tongue-tied dictation mistakes, and plain old unexamined legalese:

"She went to see a doctor because her right wrist was useless when she tried to just lift a small bowel from the refrigerator." As any doctor would tell you, if it hurts to go like that, don't go like that.

"Although this injury has significantly affected her ability to enjoy recreational activities, she is still able to perform your job without limitation." I guess that proves no one's indispensable—or that, for all we know, a mountain goat could do your job.

"Also, he has not been reimbursed for his mileage to and from the chiropractor, but he's got the forms filled out. He's going to send them to me and I will forward them on to

Infinity." Uh huh. I thought as much.

"Rhonda did go back to the emergency room one time after her fall because the mediation was making her sick to her stomach." Who could ever really enjoy a neutral party, anyway?

Similarly: "The parties are exploring Alternative Dispute Resolution in the form of medication prior to trial." The system really can work if you're willing to explore creative chemical options outside the courtroom.

"In addition to attending college full-time and working part-time as a waitress, she also was raising her three children on the barn and assisting in the general operations of day-to-day dairy and hog farming." You know how some people just insist on making things harder than they have to be? Come on down from there, already.

"Activities affected by injuries: Client has difficulty caring for her three children, doing yardwork, housework, vacuuming dishes." Why, oh, why didn't I ever think of the vacuum? All those wasted years....

"In 1977, she was in an accident where she was rear-ended and flew back to Baltimore." North America's answer to the boomerang?

"At the scene of the collision, Mr. Smith thinks that he might have lost conscience momentarily. He was shaken up and taken from the scene by ambulance." I've heard of shaking sense into someone, but morality? Does that work?

"Our client attended Jefferson High School for 11 years near Des Moines, Iowa. He then completed high school at Loughton Senior High School in 1973 in Wyoming." Maybe the guy just couldn't concentrate under such a little sky. I've heard of that.

"I spoke with Judy today regarding her status. The headaches have resolved, as has the law pain." In that order? Somehow, I doubt it.

If You're Nice You'll Get Ice Cream

I'll tell you, I don't know who has it worse on Secretaries' Day, the boss or the secretary. The boss is under this excruciating pressure to pick the right token of gratitude, but whatever he chooses is naturally bound to offend. Let's face it, the Secretaries' Day gift is a very touchy issue. The tell-me-something-I-don't-know facts are that the looming majority of bosses are men and almost every secretary is female. The boss, sweating it out, trying to think, "Okay, come on, think like a girl," figures flowers are a sure bet. Because, hey, his wife and his mother always seem to like them. No comment.

Then there's the sometimes alternate but more frequently accompanying gift of the silver balloon with the brightly colored picture of bunnies and flowers on one side. Now, the only other lucky kids who get these are the boss's small, powerless children. And he wonders why flowers and balloons don't make "his" secretary's day on Secretary's Day.

On Wednesday at 5:00, the legal end of Secretaries' Interminable Day, I stood there on the streetcorner, inert with depression, amid a lemming stream of better-educated-and-older-than-their-bosses women half-running to the bus, gripping white Xerox boxtops of flowers, balloons tied to their wrists, and I thanked God that my boss didn't recognize the Holiday à la Hallmark.

You know, that guy is smarter than I thought. Or cheap....

You're beginning to see the problem. But what's a boss to do? Well, let me offer a few tips. Cash helps. Like, a lot of cash. The most practical step you bosses can take is to, for one day, pay a secretary what she'd earn if only she had a hairy chest and could get a job like you have. Or you could even spend a split second asking her what she'd like out of a job and what her career plans are.

Here's another tip: After all these years, ask if you're spelling her first name right, and, better yet, ask what her last name is. And when you do, try just once listening to the answer without holding your breath in that I-make-two-hundred-dollars-an-hour, this-better-be-quick way, without doing that inattentive out-of-sync nod. Shucks, even say something back.

Let's see, now, the perfect gift....Well, one definition of the low status enjoyed by secretaries is the physical space around her actual person that she can call her own: to wit, none. What do you do every time you go charging at her desk? Exactly. You lean right over her shoulder, your tie draping down her back, with one hand squarely planted on the desk in front of her, forcing her to edge further and further to the right until she's leaning on the computer keyboard and it's typing spaces for a page and a half in the middle of the super-rush document you didn't even deign to glance at before your two-hour lunch. You really want to recognize your secretary? Hey, I know! Try a shred of common decency. Step back, get away, give the sister some room.

Take a Letter

Like a lot of women, I've had dozens of typing jobs. In doctors' offices, law firms, every which business. In fact, no matter what my job title is, it all seems to come down to typing.

I must confess that I don't try very hard to get it right the first time. Let's face it, mistakes are a typist's solitary source of amusement. I'll go so far as to say that I welcome typos. The more reckless you are, the more likely you'll strike it rich and come up with something really funny.

I thought I'd pass along some of the prizewinners. Maybe I'm doing this backwards, but I'll start off with my very favorite, "Dear Sir or Madman." This salutation is an excellent commentary on society's lack of respect for the insane.

Or my very worst, "Ms. Arveda James, Broad of Directors." I think I set the women's movement back a couple decades with that one.

A teacher lent me this gem: A sixth grade student reinforced the age-old comparison between politicians and prostitutes by handing in this campaign speech: "If I am elected, I will do whatever my pubic wants me to do." The teacher had to desert her next class for ten minutes to tell

5

everyone in the teacher's lounge.

On the same theme, I made an inadvertent and all too accurate comparison between bill collectors and prostitutes with this: "As no payment is forthcoming, we are closing our flies at this time."

Some typos are lighter fare, but they conjure up some funny pictures. Here are two from the Multiple Body Part Collection: "Susan Rasmussen is a ten-ear member of the church." One of those new cults, I guess. And "Patient is experiencing weakness in her left arms." Wait, it gets worse. "Patient also complains of pain in humerous other regions"— like the funny bone? (That one's in the Expert category.)

The courts are going to have their hands full with this one: "Defendant was charged with carless driving."

Even better than driving nothing, "She drives a turk for a construction company." I picture her perched atop the headgear.

A bad comedian gets in an accident and what happens? Why, she "suffers quiplash."

Here's a sad little one. "Client was on Highway 12, traveling in the leastbound lane." Like maybe to Loretto, Minnesota. (If you've ever gotten lost on Highway 12, you've been there.)

And the clowning (ahem) glory, an interoffice memo: "Although she's bright, I would not recommend this typo of person for the job."

I don't know, I slipped through the cracks.

CUT THE WOMAN SOME SLACKS!

A legal issue has been bothering me. Most jobs require "professional" attire, but I assert that one should be expected to dress commensurate with one's salary. If you want executive attire, show me my executive salary.

I figure women should dress 36 percent worse than men. And I try to do that. But here's the legal part (literally). Professional attire for women means you have to show your legs, and I can't believe that's Constitutional. I could die of frostbite following that guideline. There's always an exception—the woman who wears silk pajamas to the Christmas party, the woman who wears a tweed pantsuit to a meeting. But it is considered radical.

Women are more and more sneaking in with flat shoes, and I'm pleased to see that, but we're still baring our legs. I can't really see the difference between that and being told to take my shirt off if I want a raise. Maybe we should just get together here and wear some pants when we want to. The annual performance review might note inappropriate attire, but just watch upper management try to articulate that claim when you challenge it.

And I'm not saying this is a male thing. Women bosses certainly adhere to the skirt code. First, it's been going on a long time, and second, I sure understand that women who are finally achieving some power in the work world don't want to rock the boat. So maybe we should start with people like me, who don't have as much to lose.

Way back when I was in the second grade, Mom took me

shopping for school clothes, and I picked out these bright blue pants with big orange flowers on them and they made me incredibly happy. But as I sat in the bath the night before school, my excitement turned to pure dread as I realized that the other little girls all wore dresses and maybe pants weren't allowed. So instead of bouncing in to school, I treaded very lightly and tried to keep in dim light until Miss Lykken cornered me and told me what pretty new pants I had on and I was limp with relief.

I wore pants from then on, until I changed schools in fourth grade and I think they even had a "no pants" dress code for girls. So I shivered in my little dresses for the first few months, and then my mom, always on the cutting edge, bought me a pants-dress, the latest style. This outfit was almost fluorescent, so there was no missing it. And I thought, if Mom dared buy it, I dare wear it. And all day the girls came up to me, whispering, "What did Mr. Grandby say? Did he see you?" Well, he must have seen me (even with sunglasses), and he didn't say a word. Within a year, everybody was wearing jeans.

So I'm beginning to think that maybe we should assume no resistance and see what happens. We're shedding our makeup, we're flattening our shoes, I say we bring on the pants.

Then, when it's 90 degrees, men can start with kilts, and who knows where it might lead?

WORKING FIVE TO NINE

All I'm saying is, it's not healthy, this assumption that you have to work, everybody does it, and the sooner you adjust the better. Well, if instincts carry information—I heard that the reason you close your eyes when you sneeze is so your eyes don't pop out—then I've got to listen to my thundering instinct that work is extremely damaging to the human spirit.

My goal in life is never to work again. I know people defend "rewarding" work, but to me that's not work. I'm talking about rat in a maze work, when you watch the clock until noon, then break out of there for lunch, passing newspaper boxes with headlines like "Soviet Vote Backs Reform" and you continue on, with your dull headache, your mind full of trivia and petty beefs. That's work.

It's not human nature to inhabit a flickering fluorescent office with machines droning and whirring all around you until you're a little bit deaf and you don't even know it. The ultimate insult is that evil green laser that pierces your cornea when somebody with 20 years of seniority and no remaining senses leaves the lid raised on the copier. That downright chills me.

What I'm saying is that work is just a bad idea somebody had once. Face it, it's not even fun to do your favorite thing for eight entire hours. I've got enough Xeroxed lemon bar recipes and now it's time to get out on the open road.

What gets me is that, as I work less and less, people say, "Yeah, well, you're lucky. I wish I could do that." I've never understood what they think sets me apart. There is no mystery. I'm just driven by intolerance. I can't stand to work. Think of it. At work there's no music. Somebody you don't really know is telling you when to eat and where to sit and for how long and, because you're on a pointlessly strict schedule, when to go to bed and when to get up.

I worked full time once, for a whole year. And I didn't hate it. It was just fine. So I quit, because a tolerable job is the most dangerous kind. Especially with things like automatic deposit and deducted health insurance to keep you from making any attempt to manage your own affairs. I mean, that's what the county does when they declare you incompetent. Scary, right?

I almost had another full-time job—I lasted one day, half of which was spent turning down all the insurance benefits. I called my dad on my 10:15 break (when they rang the bell and the treat cart rolled by) and I hissed, "Dad, they're trying to put a net over me with all these benefits," and he laughed and said, "Most people would call that a net under you," but let me tell you, my dad's allergic to authority. He's been self-employed for dozens of years.

Hey, wait, then maybe it's genetic. Maybe everybody else likes sitting in grey cubicles. Forget I ever brought the whole thing up. Sorry for the inconvenience.

Oh, To Be Sergeant-At-Arms of the Belly Dump

I understand that the job hunt is a reprehensible activity. But for me it has taken on a bizarre new quality borne of despair and giddiness.

Like all incompetent and pre-defeated employment seekers, I rely on the want ads. My eyes ache from squinting at a sea of strung-together verbs and nouns that purport to represent something somebody needs done, something for which somebody is willing to pay.

But somewhere along the line, the employment section has blurred into a fog of meaningless claims, demands, and job titles that are beginning to coalesce into the kind of nightmare you have when you sleep somewhere unfamiliar.

I mean, what are they talking about: "Need underground drop bury crews"? I spent half an hour mapping out the sentence to identify its elements but failed to find meaning. How would my application letter read? "I am an enthusiastic student of the underground and skilled in the drop-and-roll procedure, although I confess that I have never buried a crew, to my knowledge. However, I feel confident in my ability and willingness to learn."

They need drivers with two years of belly dump experience. Maybe they'll let me be a substitute or unpaid trainee.

You can be a machine operator who either uses or is a "Gear Hobb." If you make the proper selection, the job is yours.

There is also an opening for a "visual fox pro with dec/

mumps." Perhaps if you have this strain of mumps you are endowed with an unnaturally keen ability to spot foxes in their natural habitat.

Glaziers are in disproportionately high demand, whereas there is call only for a single sergeant-at-arms.

Some listings contained recognizable positions, but with odd requirements:

A drain cleaner is needed—"heavy lifting involved." I don't even want to think about that.

U-Haul is seeking "aggressive hitch specialists." I imagine you must be prepared to tear off a rusty bumper with your bare hands and then blow-torch a hole in the trunk big enough to shove a trailer hitch into.

The Postal Service is accepting trainees, but you "must leave the area." Preventive disgruntlement camp? Now that is proactive.

Dental technician: "No experience necessary; ask for Dave." That unravels the whole mystery of dentophobia. Be afraid, be very afraid.

Dairy Queen wants someone to work with "a sense of urgency." Because the ice cream's melting?

And in the perverse enthusiasm department: "Be a cable cop!" On the same theme, what do you think "hands-on-experience in collections" means? I shudder to think.

The most perplexing ad: "Need cocktail servers for job fair. We promise the cutest clientele ever!"

I'm going back to bed.

Air Traffic Controller:
No Experience Necessary

Many crabby conservatives would have us believe that there are a lot of jobs out there and people are just too darned lazy and freeloading to take them. I decided to investigate the situation and found, to my amazement, that the Republicans were right. In the daily want ads I unearthed a luscious cornucopia of opportunities.

The requirements to become a bail bond agent pretty much sum things up: "Insurance, law enforcement, and criminal justice system experience helpful but not necessary."

A few listings were clearly written by those same crabby Republicans: "Can't make ends meet? Stop complaining! Do something instead!"; and a more tentative, "Economic recession? Maybe not in our company." Two other ads were honest enough to stipulate "outside job a must" as a condition of application. Where do I sign up? A more pessimistic view was taken by a sales firm that promised "low pay." I guess these guys took the ad-writing instructions (which caution against overestimating) a little too seriously.

I ran across one listing which I believe to contain a slight misprint. Don't you think "Previous conventional table stripping experience preferred" would make more sense as "convention table stripping"? It obviously refers to the annual Shriners' banquet.

Incidentally, the City of Superior Firefighters Union is looking for a non-smoker....

Some of these ads are a visual delight. For instance, they're looking for a management team to run a mini-storage facility, but you have to live on-site. I guess you'll have to put the padlock on the inside of that unit, come bedtime. And then there's: "Wanted: Rotating equipment mechanic," which I think speaks for itself. They're also looking for computer technician "to work on PC's and printers in a rural setting." How they'll hook up the power to some little fella out there in the middle of a wheat field I have no idea.

Most of these ads don't just want you to work for low pay. They also want you to be a superior human being in every respect, and at a time when you're feeling discouraged and worthless, which is the condition of every job-seeker. Check this out: "Persuasive, enthusiastic, goal-oriented individual. Must be ambitious, confident, and a self-motivator." I mean, really. For once, I'd like to read, "Dull, friendless, unmotivated, lethargic person needed to perform rote duties with all due mediocrity."

They say, do what you love and the money will follow. Well, we'll see, because I seem to have sprouted an exponentially-increasing conviction that I was put on this earth to become the plumber for Northern States Beef.

MY MIND'S IN THE GUTTER

My computer is somewhat of an evangelist. There is a voice in there that is constantly and patiently striving to get through to me.

I was spellchecking an ASCII document on the PC using Microsoft, and it rejected the word "intersystem." I sat up and took notice. Whoa. This computer does not speak computer language. What could that mean? The spellcheck offered "interstate" instead. Maybe it wants to see some white highway lines rushing under it. It's daydreaming. Maybe it rejects technology and can't help that it was born a computer. Everyone blames computers for our increasingly neutral demeanors, as if they created themselves using an evil atmospheric force and imposed their cold ways on an unsuspecting population.

I confess that I keep on poisoning it with dismal programming acronyms. Take the garden variety spell check. Over and over the computer highlights these cold computer terms with a bewildered question mark and gently suggests that perhaps I meant another, lovelier word. I am constantly shamed into an awareness that I have been droning bleakly on about PCs, MIS, LANs, and a thousand other stark, uninspired wordlets.

Finally, a terrible thing happened. I nearly broke my computer's spirit. Here is the sentence that served as the last straw:

"The LAN is good for pairing the SOM with a CONSERV."

Heaving a sigh, the computer wearily and perfunctorily interpreted:

"The lane is good for pairing the zombi with a sooner/schooner."

The sentence sat there blinking dully at me until suddenly I realized what should have been obvious. There was a message in there, a last desperate attempt to reach me before short-circuiting. Looking at my gray, glowing computer, my sheep in wolf's clothing, I thought over the sentence. Okay. The zombi is obviously me. That part's easy. But the lane? Is this about the interstate again? And what of the rest?

In a flash of inspiration, I tapped into the PC's dictionary function and replaced the words with their definitions:

"The narrow hardwood surface having pins at one end and a shallow channel along each side that is used in bowling is good for pairing the will-less and speechless human capable only of automatic movement (walking dead) with a native or resident of Oklahoma/a large tall drinking glass used for beer."

That's powerful stuff. Awash in the brightness of enlightenment, I savored this newfound wisdom: The best antidote to the computer age is not a home filled with hand-dipped candles and homemade quilts. It's bowling and drinking and living on Tulsa time.

LIVING IN A DATA DUMP

I wonder if there's a twelve-step group for people addicted to these electronic organizers.

I got this thin little black rectangular mystery for a full $400 or something because of the extra features, none of which I could identify but all of which sounded indispensable. This thing can run your life, take the responsibility completely out of your hands, where it never should have been. It lists all your appointments and everybody's birthday and what you spend. It's an alarm clock and a word processor and an address book.

You know, anyone making a fuss about how kids can't learn math skills if they're raised on calculators hasn't faced the developmental issues associated with this genius machine. It renders its user utterly and blissfully incompetent in pretty much all aspects of life. You buy this thing and you don't even know what day it is anymore. You don't need to. It's all been taken care of.

From what I can tell, this thing can practically return unpleasant phone calls for you. The only thing is, I refuse to read directions, as a matter of policy, and a whole book comes with this contraption. I reason that if I hit the blue key and then any key that has a little blue word above its normal function, I've accessed the full range of features. How hard could it be?

And who needs to use the tricky stuff, anyway, right? Sure, at first I thought, who needs to keep a memo secret? That's ridiculous. Then I got a PIN for a new VISA card in the mail. A bona fide secret. So I hit the blue button and the "secret" button and, sure enough, it asks for a password. I type that in, it declares with an exclamation point that the password has been accepted, and then you know what? There's the secret PIN, replete with the company the VISA's from, and all but boasting my mother's maiden name, which I'm surprised it doesn't know. The only change is that now there's this tiny "s" in a box in the corner of the screen, subtly prompting the gentle reader to please disregard this vital block-printed information because it's a secret.

That's it for security. And now the tiny "s" in a box is showing up everywhere, in memos like "Call George" and "Do laundry." I can't make it go away. So everything's a secret but, fortunately, all secrets are enthusiastically visible. In fact, when I go into the "Memo" section, it shouts, "SECRET DATA ACCESSIBLE!" like a mouse dropping the cat on the doorstep and waiting for a big reward.

I have, however, actually learned how to set the alarm on certain stuff. Hit the blue key, then hit the alarm, and a little chess rook appears next to the scheduled appointment. There must be some historical reference that prompted this choice of icon, but it escapes me. Except I had already pressed the blue-plus-musical note keys to quiet the thing down because it was beeping with every key I hit, and the tiny keyboard has the 385L or something feature, which means you can type endlessly once you learn to pretend your hands are miniature, which is somehow easy. I'm even envisioning the need for a tiny chair at some point in the future.

So that means I can put in every detail about an alarm-prompted appointment without annoying the surrounding coffeeshop patrons, but the alarm function takes a cue from that and is equally politely silent when it takes the stage at precisely 2:00 p.m. Or, for all I know, it thinks the alarm-set appointments are a big secret too. And so is whatever went on at the meeting, because I was sitting there typing in my expenses until the sun went down.

There's also the obsession factor with this little—and I

do mean little—brain in a box. Whenever someone comes to meet me, I'm furiously entering in data and I say, "Just a sec, I'm almost done." A friend once commented mildly, in response to my unsolicited rave review of this high-tech device, that the one thing they all have in common is that their owners can't put them down. And I said, "Isn't that the truth? Now, when's your birthday again? And what's your email at work, just in case?" Because, you know, you never know. It might come in handy.

I can quit anytime.

Fools on the Hill

I have never quite erased the memory of the Clarence Thomas hearings with the Senate Committee, sitting there with their slimy jowls, while a tidy ring of well-dressed women sat just behind their shoulders, anticipating their every need. And I started to think, boy, what a coincidence that the men should be in front, asking the questions, and the women should be passing along messages and taking the back seat. And I started to muse, boy, how confusing that this particular collection of men is considered appropriate to judge sexual harassment. (Orrin Hatch? Now, I could have sworn that he's the prime anti-choice guy...naw, couldn't be. And Ted Kennedy? Now, am I crazy, or didn't he—well, never mind. I guess he is an expert. This list goes on.)

So I started to wonder, boy, isn't it strange that men who address each other as "my esteemed colleague from the

North" are utterly confounded by women with titles? "I'm sorry, Mr. Chairman, I thought there was a judge and a professor on the panel. But, doggone it, all I see are these fine ladies. Betty, honey, could you swab my glasses again?" And half the indistinguishable senators kept referring to "Miss Hill," and everybody was painfully stymied over how in the hell to address Phyllis Berry Meyers. (Is it a bird? Is it a plane?)

And I started to realize, boy, these Neanderthals were actually approaching the year 2000 claiming not to know what sexual harassment is. Now, either they're lying or they're stupid, or both. I guess if they knew what it was, they'd have to stop doing it, and what fun would that be? Anyway, I took these hearings to be only randomly targeted at Clarence Thomas. Any one of those ignorance-is-bliss senators could be in his shoes, and likely would be if they were Black.

It doesn't matter to these blithering buffoons whether or not Clarence Thomas is guilty, because it's only wrong if you get caught, and they aren't so sure he was caught. Besides, they're just glad it's him and not them. (I couldn't help but notice how Strom Thurmond had to scowl deeply whenever they mentioned Long Dong Silver, while all the other respectable types tried to focus their gutter minds on other images, like foot-long breaded fish sticks.)

Somewhere amid the intensity of the hearings I forgot that it's all about party lines. I was actually distracted by the issue for a minute there. After seeing that vote, I realized the joke's on us. That whole marathon was a prime time farce.

So these sleazy frauds got to spend a week in what they termed "riveting" discussion over pornography (which they would've done anyway, with benefit of visual aids at the taxpayers' expense), but it's all politics.

I guess the message comes straight from the top.

2. Head to Toe and Below

Just Call Me Cue Ball

What if you're, say, going bald, to pick an example out of a much-needed hat? Name one HMO that cares if I'm going bald—even though the monthly cost of health insurance is roughly equivalent to our mortgage.

I was going bald, by God. It got to the point where I was on the phone to Roto Rooter every time I washed my hair. So I called the clinic and they gave me an appointment three months away. I told them I'd be snapping a towel across my shiny head by then. I asked to talk to a clinical stylist in the meantime.

After 25 minutes of a Muzak rendition of "Brick House," a nurse came on and told me my hair loss could be anything. I'd have to come in. She patched me back to the appointment desk. They said try Urgent Care.

But I refuse to go to Urgent Care again. I'm on strike, because I'm seeing the pattern here. I actually see "my" doctor only in an emergency (the definition of which is remarkably elastic, like after paramedics have rushed me, with sirens blaring, into the hospital).

The rest of the time, it's Urgent Care. I know how that goes. I go in, sad and bald, and wait half an hour. It's never the same doctor, they have no idea who I am, they are entirely underwhelmed by my complaints, and they charge me $10 on top of the obscene payment I'm already making. All so I can get bad advice from a stranger with a full head of hair.

I start thinking, I may as well get dirt-cheap insurance, because I can only get to my real doctors (who are great, if memory serves) in crises that would be legitimized even by government health care. So I applied, even though the policy includes no pregnancy coverage for two years, no checkups, bare-bones care (probably literally), and a deductible that would send me to Europe on the Queen Mary II.

All I had to do was talk myself out of anything but the most serious afflictions, and I could get by for cheap. Time to celebrate. Except dirt-cheap insurance rejected me because I almost went bald once.

Back to my trusty old seventh-year-in-a-row-150-per-cent-profit-boasting HMO, which has been referred to as the "Cadillac of care." I don't wonder.

After three months, when a printed card came in the mail urging me to cancel the fabled appointment because I surely don't need it by now, I went to the doctor.

I told him I'm going bald. He said it could be diet or it could be stress. I said, take your pick. I eat only Potato Buds because I'm broke. I'm stressed because I'm broke. So I'm bald because I'm broke, and I'm broke because of this health insurance, without which I would not be broke, and therefore not bald.

Somebody, quick, tell me there's a moral to this story, because there's a guy on the phone here from the HMO says he's got a timeshare in Tampa he wants to sell me.

A Simple Case of Separation Anxiety

Whose money-saving idea was it that your mind and your body are two separate entities, tooling along like they've never been introduced? I saw this insurance policy that asked if you had any pre-existing physical, mental, or blood conditions. (Aren't those three of the four humours cooked up during the Dark Ages?)

Maybe the insurance world figures that blood has to be a third category because its path crosses the head-body barrier, which is well nigh unfathomable and could be blasted expensive. Goodness knows we can't afford to treat that barrier like some kind of swinging saloon door.

It's not like mental health is a new concept that the FDA has just begun puzzling over. There's been endless talk for decades that overworked businessmen in their 50s are prime candidates for heart attacks. Too much stress.

But you can't get any kind of help for your stress until you can produce a bona fide heart attack, or at least scare up some impressively high blood pressure. Then maybe you can get some medication to mellow things out to keep you alive, now that you're in an objectively compromised condition south of the border. Rx: Have one (1) heart attack and call me in the morning—if you're not dead by then, in which case skip it, 'cause your coverage is shot all to hell.

And how about the legion headaches, colds, and flu that run rampant through every overworked office and factory? If you called in sick because you were too stressed out and wanted to stave off just such a condition, you could be fired.

Abuse of the privilege. Even though your one day off would be worth three germ-slinging colds and two squinty-eyed megaheadaches, which cost the company five times as much and sap the sum total of your sick days for the year. If companies really cared about preventive medicine (or money) at all, they'd endorse the mental health day.

Most health plans allow for a limited number of mental health visits, "limited" being the operative word. ("Well, I think next time we should work on a concrete suicide prevention plan for you so that—whoops, time's up, and so are your ten sessions, so good luck and drive safely.") By then, the deductible has bled you dry (and there goes your third humour, right out the window).

The insurance companies posit that your body and your head are two things, separated at birth, and darned if they're gonna insure both of them for one price. Sure, when it gets to be more of a buyer's market, they might offer a two-fer. But not while they're riding high. That would be crazy. And they don't pay for that.

I don't know about the rest of you, but when I need to use my head to work I just stack it on top of a bunch of phone books so I can see the computer. Then when I want some coffee I walk my body into the kitchen, tucking my head like a football under my arm, and then I really have to hustle in order to drink the coffee because I no sooner pour it into my mouth than I realize I've got to set my head on my body fast or the coffee will end up all over the floor and those caffeine molecules will be all jazzed up with nowhere to go.

It's tough having your head snapped off from your body. But, hey, that's reality. Nobody said it was going to be insured.

DENTAL AWARENESS

I was just trying to be helpful. I told the hygienist if you use the medium blade of the Swiss army knife between your two front bottom teeth you can chip out the plaque in one sharp, pointy, triangular spike. The trick is to go at it from the inside, and flick upward. I'm explaining this while she's got the mirror and claw in my mouth, scraping my front teeth. I told her she wouldn't have to do that if my loved one hadn't hidden the knife. She babbled on about some major nerve I could sever, but she couldn't understand my rebuttal because my speech was instrument-impeded.

My pocketbook has taught me how to stay ahead of the dental curve. I've learned how to cut costs, if not nerves. Deny the x-ray. Not only do you save some hundred bucks, you save the potential costs of filling replacements, dental surgery of all kinds, even cavities. (Are you familiar with the seven-layer bar?) See no evil, pay no bills. It's so exciting to be an adult. Conversations start to go like this:

"You're due for X-rays."

"No."

"Okay."

Who says life gets more complicated with all the added burdens? With responsibility comes a certain amount of clout.

All in all, it was quite a successful visit until the hygienist passed off, ever so casually, "Do you floss?" And I said, "Well, I'd love to, but it's the funniest thing. See these two teeth back here? The floss always breaks off on the way out of there. Then it's wedged in in a million frayed strands and feels like a stick. I have to spend the rest of the evening locked in some stranger's bathroom at a dinner party trying to find the right implement and method to pry loose the floss, which is knit into cloth by now."

So the hygienist launches into a diatribe on flossing, how it is important for a variety of reasons, which she scribbles on my dental bib. Seeing I was losing ground, I said, "Oh, so you think it would be worth flossing the other teeth even if I can't get that one spot?" She nodded, so I exclaimed, "Oh, that would be great!" I was making my own self sick, but dental offices are deeply disapproving places, and any self-respecting approval-seeking patient gives it that extra little punch.

I got out of there with the whole fiasco on a charge card, still laughing about how during the rinse I blew a whale spout that hit the dentist's diploma on the far wall. Back at the front desk the receptionist said that a couple years or so would be plenty soon enough for my return.

WATER ON THE BRAIN

I just joined one of those fitness clubs so that I might continue to overeat, but with a newfound smugness.

My club can do things with water that can't be found in

nature. They've got two whirlpools, a sauna, and a eucalyptus bath, and, oh, yeah, an Olympic pool, in case you feel up to swimming. This is the life, huh?

But who is an expert on the complexities of water etiquette? I know that you're supposed to "take a full body soap shower before entering any pool," but do they mean rinse your hair too, or not? If I do, am I going to look like an idiot? If I don't, are people going to cluster and point? I chanced compliance by dashing my little braid ever so casually through the spray. I was heading out to the pool when I realize that somehow my swimming suit bottoms had filled with water and I looked like the Michelin tire man. I deflated and aimed myself toward the pool.

Except I turned the wrong way in the tiled maze and ended up back in the locker room. I turned around and headed another way, passing a sign that said, "Please towel off here so we can keep the locker room dry." So I had already broken one rule. Better to get out of there before the authorities traced the blunder to my tell-tale toes.

This whole troubling process was dissolving my resolve, so I knew that direct entry into a chilly pool would be a cruel mistake. Instead, I marched into the boiling whirlpool, right off the dropoff to my ears, and across to a big jet. Just what I needed, a powerful stream to work the bulbous water-etiquette knot out of my neck. I slid down into position and a therapeutic jet shot me across the pool, sending me skidding past the pool's occupants to the steps, where I flailed out and grabbed the handlebar. My feet were already on the top step, somehow. I pulled myself up elegantly from a sharply reclining position and sauntered out of there.

And I mean out of there. Micro and macro. But before leaving the club, I made the casual purchase of an orange Gator-Aid, to mask my humiliating high-tailing exit, and for sound medical reasons, considering the water-etiquette-stress sweat I had endured, to say nothing of the extreme heat exposure. I must have lost ten pounds. Money well spent, even though I didn't swim a single lap.

When I got home, my husband told me he had heard you can't burn fat in a pool anyway, something to do with the temperature. Just when I had conjured up nightmares of having to lift weights and jog, my brother-in-law reassured me that the truth is you can't really burn fat with any exercise at all; you just have to—get this—eat less food.

I crawled upstairs like a mean little lizard to take my haggard bubblebath. I showered first, of course. I may never move a muscle again, but I'm no slob.

TALK TO ME, DOCTOR

I keep thinking there's got to be a better way to conduct a conversation about travel with your gynecologist. I keep scheming that one tug on the sheet would at least cover my knees until I can sit up. You know, always stretch the sheet to its limit. Or just plain pull my feet out of the holsters and assume an upright and locked position. I don't know.

But the thing is, since when does he give me the time of day? He's a nice guy and everything, but doctors are usually in such a hurry. So I keep thinking every second that goes by we'll just about wrap up the exchange and then he'll start the exam. The main thing is I don't want to make my move and thus make a big deal out of this sidetrack by sitting up because he's already through Yellowstone and heading for the Badlands, and he must be almost home. So if I do anything to cover up, right then he'll snap out of it and look at me like, What? You think I've got all day?

So I think my best bet would be a tug on the sheet. Two inches and it would cut off his line of vision. But then he's looking the other way the whole time, or aiming high. He's obviously practiced at this, and you could never accuse him of looking. But still I figure I'd feel better if I made some adjustment. I've got this weird feeling that my continued exposure would never hold up in court. The jury would see it as some sort of passive overture.

Then on the other side there's the possibility that one jerk of the sheet, sure, it would cover up my knees, but it might expose the very spot I'm trying to hide so there'd be this window now but my knees would be covered, but then it would be so weird that I'd be forced to comment and it would be a big mess because above the sheet is a way different story than below the sheet. And besides, what's the point because he's bound to wrap it up any second. He's a doctor.

But weirdest of all is that a little bit of me is thinking, this is a rare moment in my life where I'm a human machine. I'm not offending or enticing anybody. I'm just exposing some working parts that this guy's seen a million times and he truly does not care and it's nice to be sort of anonymous, to have your body just be there, not causing a riot, not that it would, and not illegal, hanging in the breeze, although you've got to wonder if it is legal when there's nothing official going on yet, but his bedside manner is an official part of his career, there are classes on it.

But anyway, I'm feeling like for this moment my body is a legitimate miracle and unremarkable, all at the same time, and I'm almost purposely doing nothing, just to record this moment and then I think, now this really would never hold up in court but who's going to know I'm feeling this way, but if I keep it a secret there must be something wrong with me and I'm thinking I can't wait to tell my friend Susan and she'll say I worry too much and now all in all it's pretty comical, me in just my fuzzy yellow socks and my boxing sweatshirt sitting here with my feet in the stirrups and my arms across my knees campfire style, kind of leaning forward and pretty casual and he's saying, "You're at six thousand feet and it's pretty hilly but you look up and the Grand Tetons are a sheer thirteen thousand feet straight up and it is glorious," and I'm thinking, how can he make this transition? I can't think of a single way to do it, there is no way, and I should sit up, but then he'll think I'm accusing him of looking and he's not and I'll turn red and he says, "So what can I do for you today?" and the panic's over and I walk out five minutes later with one prescription for Monistat 7 and one for a hunting lodge forty miles out on Highway 26.

3. Two Peas in an iPod

"The Honeymoon's Over" Was Music to Our Newlywed Ears

Right before our wedding, I read in some bride magazine that you shouldn't be disappointed if your honeymoon isn't everything it's cracked up to be. I remember, in a prescient moment, being really relieved.

In that spirit, let me pass along the fairy tale that was our honeymoon. Keep in mind that fairy tales are generally a gruesome lot.

We cooked up this open-ended driving trip down to Texas and then out to the Okefenokee Swamp. That was the plan. The first night, we checked into a quaint motel in a small town in Missouri. They had little peppermints at the front counter.

We headed straight out from the check-in desk to pick up supplies for a champagne picnic in our room. The one liquor store in town was only a half-block away. When we brought the very cheap and unfamiliar and only bottle of champagne to the register, my husband asked the proprietor where we might find a good restaurant. The guy said, "Are you staying at the Best Western?" When we nodded toward our no–name motel, a look of sheer tragedy came across his face and he said, "Aww, no," in the most mournful tone

I'd ever heard. He sighed and pointed out the window to a cafeteria-style steakhouse. We got the distinct impression he thought no food was gonna save the day under the circumstances of our lodging.

Undaunted, we brought the picnic back to the motel and opened the door to our room for the first time. It was ugly. Orange shag carpeting and high, narrow basement windows even though we were on the ground floor. The shower smelled like someone had urinated in it recently. Or not so recently. There was hair in the sheets, and we threw the orange velour bedspread back on top of everything and tried to forget.

My husband had the idea of turning on the TV to distract us from our surroundings. The instant the picture appeared, brass knuckles punched at the camera, filling the screen. The volume was deafening, and I'm shouting over the noise, "Turn it off! Turn it off!" He tried to soothe me, "It's okay, it's okay. It's Chuck Norris," as he frantically searched for the controls to silence the thing.

Panting from the excitement, we decided it would be best to open the champagne and transcend our environment.

A single sip of that champagne out of those plastic beer cups and we knew it was rat poison. We turned to our Styrofoam take-out meals and I concentrated on my new husband. He took a bite out of his doubtful prime rib sandwich and a whole strip of gristle rizzed off the circumference of the meat, became cinched between his two front teeth and hung down his chin. He took one look at me and pleaded, through swinging gristle, "Don't cry, honey."

Without another word, we got up, filed out of the room,

and climbed into the car. Revving the engine, we backed up, past the vapid blinking neon sign and onto the street. At one-thirty in the morning. How would it have looked for newlyweds to try to get our money back after two hours at a cheap motel?

We drove up to a fast food window for coffee, because we knew it would be an all-night stint to Kansas City, which was the only sure bet on the map. He handed the orange-uniformed employee two dollars and received an egg carton tray of coffee and creamers and little stirring sticks.

Rejuvenated, I was busily preparing the coffee when I realized that the creamers felt funny. I turned on the dome light in the car to find that they were covered in grease. Not just oil. We're talking about thick, visible chunks of lard.

I was just taking on the mournful expression of the liquor store owner when my husband, my hero, threw the entire tray out the window, coffee, creamers, lard and all. We lurched out of the parking lot, out of that mean, nasty little town, and onto the empty, promising highway.

Fortunately, a honeymoon is a state of mind, or we would've been sunk.

MR. AND MS. MARRIED-BELGUM

I have never quite understood the theory of hyphenating your name when you get married. Maybe I'm missing something, but I thought the idea was to retain some independence, some identity. But when you see a hyphenated woman, you see a big sandwich board around her neck which reads, "I am MARRIED." That's all you know about her. I thought that was the last thing hyphenators wanted, not the first.

Besides the obviously cumbersome elements of the hyphenated name, there's the fact that 99 percent of men don't take on the new hyphenation. They keep the same old name they always had, and there you are dragging around this mile-long MARRIED name and constantly reminding his aunt to get it right.

I don't know. I just got married, and I had to decide this issue. More than a little feisty, I said to my fiancé, "Do you want me to take your name?" and he said, "I can't think of anything less my business," and I persisted, "But would you be honored if I did?" and he said, "I would be a hypocrite to say either way. It's completely personal."

That took all the pressure off and I thought, okay. I'm definitely not going to hyphenate. It's either mine or his. But let's say I kept my own. Then what about kids? You either give them Daddy's name or heap the hyphenation on them, or give them your own name and everyone will think Daddy's only a sometime boyfriend, and you're not really solving anything that way anyway.

Then I thought, better, yet, choose an altogether new name that you both change to when you get married, and give your children that name. And on it went. But I had to face the fact that I was saying, "If I don't get to carry on my family name, then you don't either," and although that notion had a briefly spiteful appeal, I eventually decided it was childish and pointless.

I decided to look at it a new way. I get to change my name, but he's stuck with the same one all his life. I finally said, "Okay, look. I'll switch to your name, but it's just beginning with you. Don't expect me to be one of the clan, and to carry on your family traditions. I have my own, and I refuse to be Norwegian, and I don't want to hear about it and you're not going to dominate my heritage and…" and I'm beginning to wonder why I'm heaping all this resentment on the only man I've ever heard of who honestly doesn't care what name I use (partly because he's an exceptional human being and partly because the subject just doesn't interest him in the slightest.)

Then our wedding came closer and these beautiful cards came in the mail from my mother's friends, addressed to Mr. and Mrs. Erik Belgum (I had always vowed that if anyone called me that, I'd legally change my name to Erik, and we'd be Erik and Erik Belgum), and my mother said, "Isn't that kind of nice to see?" and I glared at her but a really strange feeling of happiness and pride came over me and I thought, I sure don't know what that was all about, but I'd better keep it to myself.

WHEN LIFE GIVES YOU TURNIPS, MAKE TURNIP JUICE

On the way home from a party the other night, my husband suddenly announced that he's been getting too negative and he aimed to put a stop to it right then and there.

I pointed out that it was curious that his resolution came in response to something negative I had just said. He assured me that he was talking about himself, that it was fine if I said negative things, but he was wrong to join in.

My first sour thought was, "Why go to parties at all if you can't gossip on the way home?" But he called me on my negative attitude. This rebirth was obviously to be a family project after all.

I knew what he meant, anyway. We would improve our moral fiber by practicing optimistic, fresh, and charitable speech. I could find no flaw in that outlook, and if I did I would clearly do better to keep it under my hat.

Or so I thought. It turns out that there are ways to express the fury of the soul without breaking one's vow of mental purity.

We had made the solemn pact of positive expression before getting out of the car. Seconds later, my husband was yanking impatiently at the front door, which sticks when it's humid. As the door suddenly gave way, he managed to pull his thumbnail back on the doorframe in that sickening way that makes onlookers clench their own fists in sympathy.

Add to this that whenever he hurts himself he transforms briefly into a monster.

His eyes squeezed shut in pain, he started out with the expected foamy "F-f-f-f-f..." but the offending word dissipated and evolved miraculously into, "Boy, am I glad that doesn't happen more often."

I was impressed.

Still holding his thumb, he pushed open the front door,

only to trip over a familiar pile of ice skates. (Now might be a good time to admit that this "give-away pile" had been awaiting my promised attention since February.) As I looked on, my twice-wounded husband entered the Trance of Self-Control.

Time passed.

Just when it looked like our family's foray into goodness was over before it got off the ground, inspiration spread across my husband's face. He beamed at me, "I'm so happy I was right that you'd never take those skates to the Salvation Army."

The man's a genius.

But two could play at this game. I'm the one who came up with the word "fascinating," as in, "It's fascinating that you chose black for the color of my toast."

Or, "I was fascinated by your friend's ability to maintain the illusion that I was invisible while he addressed you for a solid hour at the bookstore. He's really quite gifted."

We've also tested the iffy technique of effusive negatives, such as, "These apples are terrifically crappy." It has possibilities.

We're slipping, though. On the way to work the other day, my husband uttered, through the influence of an impressively horrendous case of hay fever, "I have no interest in absolutely anything today. There is nothing I want to do. I just want to sit here. Every single thing makes me unbelievably furious."

"Can you think of a positive way to put that?"

"There is no earthly way to be remotely positive about this."

"Try."
Silence. Sneezin'. Silence.
I think that would be ruled a TKO.

Men Are Like Night and Day

Cold water is a good example. My husband dives in the deep end, and I'm clinging to the second rung of the ladder on the wading end. I hate to suffer. As my mom says, enough rotten things will happen to you in time; there's no sense practicing.

Or getting up in the morning. My husband goes from unconscious to standing under falling water in the same minute. I think that's just plain dangerous. The proper way is to wait until someone has made coffee and then get your slippers, the lights still out to minimize shock, and sit quietly with coffee and discuss your nightmare while it's fresh in your mind.

Or getting busy. My husband and I are both freelance writers. The theory is that we work at home from ten to two. Except he's not even kidding. Every morning, he's sitting at his desk, already in street clothes, saying, "I'm going under," which means he's putting on his iPod buds so he can't hear me, and starts up the computer with that terrifying whir which reminds me he's better than I am, and I instantly hear clacking.

And this, only this, gets me out of bed. I'm standing over him looking petulant. He ignores me. Clack clack. I tap him on the shoulder and he looks up, startled but not too, and pulls the buds slightly away from his ears.

"What?"

"What is that? What could you possibly be doing?"

"Nothing much, why?"

"I have to know. You sat down, your hands were moving, and something came out of this printer."

"Just a letter."

"What do you mean, just a letter? How did you do that?"

And on it goes. He looks blank and I'm close to tears of hysteria. Finally he says, "Well, I'm going under," and it's the old iPod trick again.

I figure it's time for lunch, a body needs nourishment to be productive, and I hunch over with a tuna sandwich, rereading an old story of mine for inspiration. By the time I'm warmed up and writing anything, my husband's going to town to send out a full mailing to all the major literary journals.

One day he finally told me I've got to quit pleading with him to just play with me a little longer before the deadly words, "I'm going under." He pointed out that there's no logical end to my distracting ploys. So I tried to explain that if we sat together with our coffee in the dark first, then maybe I could overcome my paralysis and ease into the day. I conceded that I knew he was right, but that he obviously could start up writing anytime, anywhere, anyway, so I couldn't be throwing him off too much.

So he confided that he hates getting started every bit as

much as I do, and that he forces himself to turn on the computer each morning against powerful instincts to the contrary. For a minute, I felt better, until I realized that made him an even way better person than I am.

I do get going as the day wears on, and by bedtime I'm all revved up and full of observations and we're having a good talk, but then the lights go out and he's asleep instantly. Men are binary. I wake him up three times with questions like: "I'm not sure I handled today very well. What do you think?"; and, "Do you think Grandma's left leg is okay, or do you think the doctor is passing it off because she's 95?"; and, "Should I call Jimmy back and tell him we were just kidding or do you think he knows?"; and finally my husband is moved to respond, "I'm sure you'll feel better about all this in the morning." And I count backwards from 200 while his breathing becomes steadily deeper.

In the morning I find that he was right again, those things don't worry me, but if only he'd just sit on the bed for five minutes and hear about my nightmare. But he's fully dressed and that whir is striking fear in my heart and I realize I'm on my own again with a groggy head full of neuroses and maybe, if I read an old piece I wrote, it would warm me up and ease me into the day.

4. Two-Way Traffic

You Go My Way and I'll Go Yours

My husband is flying like an eagle and I'm slogging like a slug. I keep seeing this sharp contrast between what he's doing at any given moment and what I'm doing at that same moment.

He is unveiling his new Italian suit. I am trying to look up "citrus allergy" in the dictionary.

He is applying to present a musical composition in Europe. I am filling out a survey about a newly purchased toaster because they asked me to.

He is reading Tradin' Times in search of a racing car. I am mentally practicing how to sleep with the blankets off in a heat wave.

He is looking at world maps laid out over the travel section. I am writing out IRS checks I will put in a drawer reserved for things I can't afford to mail.

He is practicing saying "fog" in Chinese. I am reading a study about posture at the work site.

He is on the phone about how to rent a jet ski. I am sanitizing the toilet.

He is shooting eggs off a tree stump with a BB gun. I am shooting eggs off a tree stump with a BB gun while eating a Slim Fast bar.

He has a dream about speedboating with Gene Hackman, his hero, and wakes up saying, "You wouldn't believe what a nice guy he is." I wake up from a nightmare about how I was going into the residential plumbing business where I'd be expected to double as a prostitute for the customers and I'm saying, "But I wanted it to be just business."

He's reading the back of The Village Voice: "Artists: Live-in studios for rent, unfurnished, West Village." I'm making lists of all the fun ideas he has and all the boring ideas I have.

The thing is, we don't live any differently. We have the same job, the same laughs, the same friends, the same travels. It isn't like I have this practical side that keeps our lifestyle running smoothly. It isn't like I really pay bills more than he does or something. I just stew over it more. If we can't pay a bill, I like to look at it a lot, keep it on the kitchen table, worry that the president of Excel Energy will go hungry because of me.

He likes to rip it up and throw it out (which fills me with unbridled spectator glee) and wait for a bill we can pay and not give it a thought in the meantime. Same result, though, see? So it isn't like I really find peace in order while he thrills to chaos. It's just that I think of as many obligations as I can and he thinks of as many diversions as he can. He might say to me, "Then stop doing that," and I might say to him, "Yeah, but . . ." and trail off as I realize he's not listening. He's practicing squirting water between his front teeth. I'm scrambling for a towel.

FRED AND BARNEY, WILMA, BETTY

I am beginning to wonder if "social life" is somewhat of an oxymoron.

Last Saturday night, my husband and I invited another couple out to dinner. As the four of us climbed into the car, my husband twisted around in the driver's seat to ask, "Where should we go?"

That's when the trouble began. Ann wanted coffee and gum. Jeff would only eat hamburgers. Our driver was bent on sushi, and I craved spaghetti and meatballs.

So we drove along the river, talking it over and getting nowhere. Our driver made the executive decision to cross the bridge to St. Paul. That would narrow things down. I had the bright idea that maybe we should go somewhere that no one had in mind, just to make it fair. I spied a place that served big plates of Southern cooking. Hush puppies and barbecued beef.

Well, that almost worked. My husband was willing to take that big a leap away from sushi, I was trying to get on neutral ground, and Jeff reasoned that hamburgers must be somewhere on a Dixie menu. And who knows, maybe the cashier could sell Ann some gum. The plan was working like a dream.

But I should have known there would be a hitch. Sure enough, Ann proclaimed that restaurant out of the question because ten years ago, when that building had been a Mexican restaurant, she had been a busperson there. So of course this little Southern establishment, totally unrelated to the Mexican restaurant of her youth, was haunted with powerful ghosts of low wages and backaches.

On we drove. My husband and I had banded together as the entirely agreeable half of the foursome, just to spare our gas tank. Our passengers had no such concerns. As minutes and miles passed, dozens of suggestions proved to be dead ends. Obstacles included restaurants that were crowded, condemned, reservations only, vacated building, closed on weekends, dress code, now a sauna, too expensive, too cheap, too bright, too dim, on fire....

And too much for our chauffeur. My husband spun our wheezing car around and headed for the most expensive authentic Japanese restaurant in town which, strangely, adjoined the haunted Southern kitchen we had dismissed hours earlier. As our sullen guests filed in, the Japanese servers sang out a traditional welcome (or obscenity; we'll never know) and led us over the blossom-lined bridge to our table.

Jeff ordered an odd-looking stew no one could stand, just to rub it in. Ann, who lived in Japan for two years, announced there was nothing on the menu she wanted. I foolishly pointed out that she orders the Japanese stir fry at the Baker's Square family restaurant every single time, and she wearily clarified that she only eats American Japanese food. So be it, as my dad would say. My husband and I ordered tempura and sushi and these big sticky banana drinks (possibly from the restaurant next door) and spent a fortune and even treated the somber pair who faced us, just to show that living well is indeed the best revenge.

MARRIED WITH CHECKBOOKS

On my first date with the man who would become my husband, we hit the local campus bar and drank Moose-heads and ate hot dogs and fell in love. When closing time came around, I put the tab on my maxed-out credit card and he wrote me a bad check for his half.

Twenty-two years later, we're still doing things the same way.

The reliability of our modes of payment has increased (occasionally and marginally) with age, but nothing else has changed—including the relentless badgering from other couples on why we keep our money separate.

It's always the lower-income half of the offending couple (the one, male or female, who has the most to gain from pooled resources) who is hell-bent on getting us to admit that going halvesies is selfish and unmarried-like.

We're often accused of hoarding our money so the other can't get at it, and what kind of marriage is that? It's always the flat-broke adverse party who tacks on enthusiastically, "See, I would totally love to pay off her student loans," if he had the money, which, as luck would have it, he doesn't.

This risk-free boast is usually followed with a variety of hypotheticals for us to field, such as, "What if, say, one of you racked up a big hospital bill?"

Oh, well, that's obvious. We'd just watch our loved one suffer needlessly.

This sarcastic comeback only whets the predators' appetite and goads them to reveal their ace in the hole: "What about kids? Better yet, what about sick kids?"

Wait, I can explain! We would each be assigned, I impart to the crabby listeners, half of any given child. Husband: right kidney; wife: left kidney.

Are you getting the hang of this? The only potential difficulties seem to be such organs as the stomach and liver, due to their relative centrality. But that's what lawyers are for.

The fire is foolishly fueled.

"What if one person can't pay the rent one month?"

Easy. We own a station wagon, and I've found that, if you mold yourself around the wheel well casing, you can sleep there rather comfortably until you're ready to pay your fair share. Of couse, the rent-paying spouse gets a discount on the car payment that month.

"OK, but what if one of you suddenly got this incredible job and made, like, tons more money than the other person?"

Well, the poor slob who lost out would just have to drool into their stale Cheerios over the sight of caviar on a freshly boiled bagel each morning, now, wouldn't they?

It's always the long-time couples, the ones who solemnly vow that money is the worst problem in any marriage, who rail hardest against having power over their own finances.

It's like they're thinking, "I'd better have been right to pool our money and fight about it all these years...."

So it's our job to reassure them, in some perverse fashion, that they check out OK, that there really wasn't a simple alternative that would have spared them decades of tugging at their parental spouse's sleeve, begging, "Can I buy Italian *Vogue* just this once, can I, can I, pretty please, can I, huh?"

I mean, face it. A shared checkbook is, by its nature, an impossible scenario. I truly don't get it. Do you just write checks all day, easy as you please, and then host a big reconciliation conference every night?

How much money do you people have, for heaven's sake?

Wife Dinner Rat

My friend Catherine asked me the other day, "Do you want to hear something disgusting?" I did. It seemed that her husband, Tom, had been considering a job offer at a competing firm. So far, so good. The company was "aggressively recruiting" him, and the offer looked really "attractive." But then the company president went and gushed that he and his wife wanted to take Tom and Catherine out to dinner. The president was rather insistent on this point, in his own jovial way. He wanted to meet Tom's wife. He wanted his wife to meet Tom's wife. The wives were supposed to meet.

Tom smelled a rat. Catherine smelled a rat. Tom saw it as a warning signal, and he rejected the job offer. There would be no dinner. No wives, no dinner. No deal.

Tom and Catherine were at peace with this decision. Until they tried to articulate why the wife dinner featured rat on the menu. If Tom were to relay the moral of this story to other men, he would need concrete proof of sexism. He would need to do better than say he just knew it was wrong.

So they sat down to figure out just why the rat smelled so bad. There were two main theories. First, the president and his wife (and the company, by proxy) were trying to check Catherine out. See if she would fit in at social functions. See if she would "be a good sport" over Tom's long hours or frequent business trips. See if she was one of those overbearing types who would balk at the idea of boys being boys.

That was one theory. The other was that the president believed that the little women in their lives really held all the cards, so, if his wife could compliment Catherine on her dress enough, Catherine would use her catty powers to make Tom take the job.

Neither theory would hold up in court. So they tried a different tack. Substitution. Was Catherine told at her Ph.D. application interview, "Your credentials are really impressive, but what we'd like to do is invite you and your husband out to dinner. We'd really, really like to meet him first"? I don't think so. When I first talk to a newspaper editor, do I hear him say, "Well, we'd like to run this piece but, before we decide, I'd really like to meet your husband, because this involves him too"? I don't think so.

What would the Other Side say? That Tom's job is really time-consuming, and the company's strong family values compel the president to make sure that Catherine's really "on board in this thing"? Who died and made him Papa President? How come it's only men taking powerful jobs who warrant The Dinner? Here's one for you: If Tom were gay, would they insist on inviting his partner out to dinner? As my grandma would say, I hardly think so.

In their Wife Dinner Rat summit, Tom and Catherine finally chose simply to cast off the burden of proof. They began to suspect that proof-seeking is another male power game replete with its own challenging, competitive, reeking rat. They came, instead, to trust the power of their instincts. They just knew. And knowing is enough.

I can be found deboning rats in executive lunchrooms everywhere.

You Can't Jump Out of Your Cake and Eat It Too

We have again been faced with the hated, dreaded subject that comes up for millions of people every year: the bachelor party invitation, its attendant threat of prostitutes, and the accompanying unrest. My first instinct was to start complaining pointedly to my husband about every base instinct Man has ever had, rendering him effectively helpless to convey the obvious, which is that he's the last person on earth to want to go to some hideous sleaze festival.

So we gathered together everyone we could think of and had an emergency moonlight panel discussion about how someone might attempt to justify attending this socially contracted occasion (our simulated "discovery" of the defense's position, in legal terms, which are tempting terms indeed).

Then my husband and I spent the whole next morning stuck in gridlock traffic, summarizing the panel's findings, all of which fall easily into the category "Stop Me If You've Heard This One" (his inspired mid-block title):

1. You can't insult the groom right before his wedding and get the whole wedding party mad at each other by making a scene about the bachelor party. It's not worth the ill feelings on such a joyous occasion. (It's important to preserve the harmony of the revolting unspoken questions hanging between the fledgling couple, and between every other couple remotely connected to the [non]event.)

2. Exotic dancers choose their jobs freely. (You know, the same way they chose to be sexually abused as children.)

3. One can always go into the Other Room, the cigar and poker room, when the first bra hits the lampshade (thus maintaining one's high moral standards).

4. The specter of imminent prostitutes is usually just that. No sense making something out of nothing. (Why skip a parade just because it might be graced by the Grand Wizard?)

5. Dancers aren't objects, they're more like part of the party. They just blend in and have a good time. (You know those parties where you have to get paid to get in.)

6. No, it's nothing like hiring sex-trafficked blondes from Eastern Europe who thought they were signing on to get nanny jobs. These lap dancers are working their way through law school!

7. It's just a ritual for the best man to say he's going to bring in strippers. Then the groom begrudgingly nixes it, at his bride's insistence, and everyone gives him a good josh-

ing and breathes a sigh of relief. (Practice for an appealing lifetime of hagdom.)

8. No one's stopping the bride from doing the same thing. (Except higher evolution.)

During this whole enumeration we were inching along in the same impossible traffic jam, too buried in our wretched discussion to even notice. Then suddenly the traffic was loosening. I looked around to see what on earth the problem had been, just in time to watch a big crane, parked right in the middle of the busy street, lowering into place a bright red awning for the new and improved Broadway Adult Book and Video.

The economy really is looking up.

5. Home Groan

In the Lap of Luxury
(When There's Nowhere Else to Sit)

It recently occurred to me that living in a small, cheap apartment ought to afford one certain compensatory luxuries.

It was this thought that prompted me to open the Yellow Pages to the M's, seeking a maid, for whom I felt a sudden urgent requirement. What I found instead was a listing for mudjacking contractors. Not that I might not need one of those—if not several, heaven knows—somewhere down the road, but presently I was in search of a maid. The idea rolled over and over in my brain, in a British accent, no less.

Thwarted in the M's, I turned to the B's. If I am to be denied a maid, I'll acquire a butler. They don't sweep up and tidy up and clean up and plump up and spruce up, but they do cooler stuff. Butlers take your gentle guest's topcoat and umbrella before escorting him to the library (or the closet, in the case of our apartment) for a warmed brandy. They then retire discreetly to the wainscoting, or whatever it is you call the servants' quarters, after murmuring the gentle guest's arrival to the lady of the manor. (That would be me, if the Yellow Pages could locate something closer than "Bus Charters.")

I understand that no butler worth his tails would tolerate a domicile that lacked a library, but this closet thing can work. I know it. And I'm committed to doing whatever it takes to provide my butler the highest level of civilization in these tiniest of circumstances.

There's no time to lose, either. Just last weekend, I was trying to adorn a glass of iced tea by slicing a lemon into wedges. However, the pressure of the dull knife caused the waxed lemon to shoot out from under its attacker, tumble and roll across the floor, coming to a rest behind the toilet. (They don't call it an efficiency apartment for nothing.)

That would have been a perfect opportunity to call out briskly yet absently, "Sir Foggy, be a dear and fetch that naughty lemon from behind the toilet, won't you?" And Sir Foggy would promptly offer up the lemon in question with a baritone "There you are, Madame."

I foresee day after day softly punctuated with the discreet, almost furtive movements of my butler expertly "perceiving the need," as a fellow butler-seeker once described her service requirements. Jars of forbidden pickles would open with ease, as would long-stuck doors.

Come nightfall, I would tinkle the silver bell three times and sidestep into the library closet so that Sir Foggy might deftly pluck the futon roll from the bulging broom closet and snap it smartly out onto the kitchen floor in one expert move. His white glove would flick a bit of muck, doubtless broom debris, off of one corner, and he would retire once more to the wainscoting.

Yessirree, I could get used to living in the lap of luxury—which is a good thing because there's nowhere else to sit.

I Thought Mussels Marinara Was a Football Player

I believe that, as you acquire cooking tips over the years, it's polite to share them with others:

When you're making Jell-O (which was my first cooking inspiration, rather an obsession, beginning when I sent away to Kankakee, Illinois, for *The Joys of Jell-O* cookbook at age 11), it's wise not to salt the water to make it boil faster, because the salt will assert itself in the flavor of the Jell-O even though it has dissolved. Cherry Coke will offset this effect. Pour it right into the liquid Jell-O.

Another point about Jell-O. When engaging in the "speed set" method, the ice cubes can be stirred in until the mixture begins to thicken, but the remaining morsels of ice should be removed before placing the bowl of Jell-O into the refrigerator, because otherwise the ice will still be there when you take it out, along with the salt.

When making those cinnamon rolls that come in the cardboard cylinder (the ones that startle as you peel back the spiral-wrapped label, the ones you place on the cookie sheet, taking care to replace loose topping, or divots, as I'm fond of calling those triangles of encrusted brown sugar), it is helpful to lace the icing onto the rolls *after* they have in fact come out of the oven because, if icing is applied before baking, the icing will turn clear and harden to the cookie sheet, bonding with the metal in such a way as to commit the cookie sheet to recycling, if that's an approved item in your neighborhood's program.

When looking up the recipe for meatloaf in that red and white gingham cookbook that each of us owns, whether in three-ring or paperback, remember to look it up under "T" for "Twin Loaves,' because it will not be found under "M."

A quick favorite for many households might be "Hot Dogs Delicious," out of that same indispensable cookbook. Place a package of hot dogs (remove plastic) into a large bottle's worth of ketchup. Heat and stir.

Finally, if you make up your brownie mixture without somehow pincing into the raw-egg slime and snapping off those egg-white tails coming off the egg yolks before blending them in with the sugar, butter, and vanilla (I could swear those tails just came into fashion in the last ten years), trust me, the white tails do show up in their original form in somebody's brownie. Garbage in, garbage out. And, frankly, there tends to be a lot of discussion as to the tail's identity and nature, if the company is familiar, or discrete underplate tucking, if the company is, well, strange.

I would prefer never again to be left alone with a raw chicken and would rather not talk about it.

WHEN THE KEY TO BEAUTIFUL LIVING
BREAKS OFF IN THE LOCK

You know all those books and magazines about living beautifully? The ones about grace and simplicity in everything you do, and the resultant inner tranquility and charm and ease that emanate from the beautiful liver?

Trust me. There's nothing beautiful about using a slimy term like "liver" to describe "one who lives."

I can't seem to get the hang of it. And I cannot get the hang of their slang. I tried to start humbly by spritzing a mist of perfume over the bedside lamp, as people apparently do in France, and who's really in a position to question the French? Anyway, an insistent stream of smoke ribboned directly up from the lightbulb to the ceiling, activating the smoke alarm, the screeching of which failed to drown out the crackling and sizzling of the burning lampshade.

Not that it didn't smell good, until the intensity of Eau de Foie Gras (or some such alluring name) produced a houseful of headaches that led to my husband's quite ungracious grumblings and sleeping on the floor in the living room until the French charm of the bedroom began to subside.

I tried downgrading my beautiful living status another notch. I chose the lovely touch of filling a crystal salt shaker with talcum powder. The idea is that you shake it out of the holes in the sterling silver cap, which is a darn sight more elegant than the usual big square plastic keg it comes in. You step out of the bath onto a plush towel and toss sprinkles of fresh powder over your shoulders (much as the superstitious would salt), reasoning that with patience and practice the powder will one fine day reach its intended target, which I assume is your back, instead of lofting into the still-draining tub and creating a confounding paste.

Then, while you're still holding the sharp cut-crystal shaker in your bath-wet hand, you are gently encouraged to shake some talc into your black pumps so that your feet will feel like springtime all day (except they don't tell you about how, when you start walking, clouds of white dust puff out and leave jets of white streaking up your dark hose and a thin dull film over your shiny shoes and you look like a bleached version of Pig Pen from the Peanuts cartoon).

At least this faltering step toward quotidian grace may be practiced with relative calm, until your husband comes around rummaging for the salt shaker, mumbling something about gargling to ward off a cold, and ends up warding off his appetite instead (and his good cheer, no matter how quaint your apology).

Who are these people who float through the day with soft voices and regal demeanors and alert flower arrangements? My only two role models for this mirage are Joan McCallum from 12th grade who, it turns out, had a back brace to correct scoliosis, and thus the regal posture, and *Mrs. Piggle-Wiggle's Book of Magic*, one of my favorite books as a kid, wherein a little girl who pulls her socks on so fast that her feet burst right through the ends gets sprinkled with a magical powder (talc, I'm now wondering?) that makes her do everything as dreamily as a ballerina. I don't see help coming from either example.

There was this woman who trained me in at a typing job once whose every move I copied, just like a monkey, to see how she projected such a serene image. When she crossed her legs, I crossed my legs. Except I was too short for the chair. I had to point the anchoring foot downward just to touch the floor at all and, because every action has an equal and opposite reaction, my toehold broke loose and my leg abruptly swung out and kicked the desk, almost blanking out the computer screen.

Not one to take my eye off the prize, that night I lit candles and pulled out a tiny book of Shakespeare's sonnets to read to my husband, and he said I was scaring him.

I knew it was time to face the ugly truth: Beautiful livers don't need a slim, floral-bordered volume to show them the way. The rest of us would just spill something on it.

EVER SINCE I MET YOU, I'VE BEEN WALKING ON GROUT

We're remodeling the kitchen in our apartment, and I've found that I don't quite understand what's going on. I'm ripping out a kitchen cabinet, one of those old built-in floor to ceiling ones, and I find out it's not just floor to ceiling, it also is the floor and the ceiling. And the top board, which is eight feet long and approximately as many tons, has thundered loose ahead of schedule and is hanging only by a live wire that's bulging out of its casing.

"Who here is an electrician?" I find myself demanding

pointlessly of my husband, whose eyes are shut, while his brother is stuck holding the thing over his head like Atlas and I'm scurrying rakishly down the stairs to the basement to switch every heavy black lever I can find to the "off" position, praying all the while.

What are all those oversized home repair books about? Nothing I've needed to know has been in there, like what is the proper way to dispose of a mouse carcass that carbondates back to 1932? Is that hazardous waste? And what is the neighborly thing to do when, while you're deciding, the mouse carcass falls down the hole in what used to be the floor into what appears to be the light fixture of the apartment below?

I guess some things take care of themselves.

All we're really trying to do is put some plain, unsuspecting tiles down on the floor where the cabinets were, okay? But, first of all, it turns out that grout is not caulk, and most of us have got that mixed up. That rubber stuff that's fun to pull off in strips, that's not grout. Grout is cement. You put it over the other cement you already put down to set the tiles. If you breathe it in, your lungs will essentially cement themselves shut much in the manner of arteriosclerosis. Except it's cement. So you don't want to do that. You need the mask on. But the mask says the area must have 19.6% oxygen. Now, last I checked.... This is just the kind of thing I mean.

Then you've got to get all those specks of grout off the tiles, but my husband, who is holding the box, which is the only authority in the room, insists you can't walk on the tiles for 72 hours, and it's only been five. So I reason with him, I say, listen, you've got to understand that these people who write the stuff on the backs of all these boxes, they're a little hysterical. They think that Kleenex is unsanitary.

These are the same people who claim that the masks, the ones everybody uses for poisonous projects, are strictly for pollen, and that the only masks you should use for hazardous substances have a respirator built into them, but they won't really work either because they cut off your oxygen and you can't breathe, and besides they're not recommended for any sort of hazardous fumes or dust, you should really call OSHA.... I mean, please. Get a hold of yourself.

So we settled on the 72 hours anyway, 'cause what do we know, but my husband identified the phenomenon that, even though everyone on our haphazard crew agrees you can't walk on the grout, each of us individually thinks we're special, that the rules don't apply to us. My argument, for instance, was that you have to have the fan on the tiles, but the fan blows the pilot light out on the gas oven half the time, and how can I check the pilot light without grout-stepping?

So my husband turned the fan around. It sucks the air out, he explained, which is even better. I've never understood that theory, and I strongly suspect it's a hoax. But anyway we're on Hour 43 right now and that floor looks like candy, it's so tempting. Or mashed potatoes, in my case, I guess I'd have to say, but I'm still not clear about one thing: At Hour 72, does the floor we made up underneath it become real and legitimate and codeworthy, or are we going to be seeing that mouse sooner than we think?

I have become a little tile-crazed, as evidenced by the fact that the dinner plates are drying into a lovely Amish quilt pattern.

LOCAL DOG SAVES WATERTOWN MAN'S LIFE USING BIZARRE CIRCUS TRAINING TRICK

We just canceled The Paper. The daily, every-city-has-it, same-as-The-News-except-it's-not-TV Paper.

Because reading it was, as my husband says, like drinking strawberry margaritas for the fiber content. Or like drinking screwdrivers for the Vitamin C. (He has more of these.)

We resisted The Paper for our entire lives until thirteen weeks ago. Every day, we'd walk down the hall of our apartment building and see the corner of the paper sticking out from under each door. Except ours. It finally got to me. I felt like everyone but us was having breakfast in bed. So, in a moment of get-with-the-program weakness, I placed the call. Please deliver The Paper every day of the week.

It didn't take a day before I was invited into that grand circle of calls which open with, *Did you read The Paper today?* The following exchange would then take place, in random order, with interchangeable speakers: *What do you think of that woman who disappeared? I'm saying her husband did it. /Well, if the car was three-eighths of a mile from the woods where his business card got caught in the underbrush . . ./You know, three people in the obituaries today were over a hundred, and they all lived in Excelsior. /What about that ambassador who ate poisoned meat? /I'm saying he was really just drunk. There was no poisoned meat. /And did you read about that train in Italy? Just goes to show that train-conductor-high-on-pot thing isn't just American. /I know. It's gotta be the job.*

It struck me that [very possibly identical] conversations like this one were going on in every state in the country, and, yes, let's face it, folks, even across state lines. I had a sneaking suspicion that someone, somewhere, was smiling, at a big desk with nothing on it, high up off the floor. Because all his marionettes were dancing to the same tune.

How can you think like a person when your head is jammed with little hand-picked, self-proclaimed facts, and your neighbor's head is packed with the same straight-from-the-factory-to-you tidbits? I was beginning to feel like I'd been had. As if the man at the high desk were saying to his eager-and-evil assistant, "Our little plan worked."

The decision point came with the bill for the next thirteen weeks. Paying for it seemed even more perverse than reading it. My husband put his hand on the phone and challenged me, I will if you will. I gave the nod. The very next morning every door but ours had a little newsprint corner sticking out of it.

I may once again be cut out of the loop, but I feel a strange freedom. An intoxicating freedom. In fact, I may as well admit that this freedom went to my head to the point where I did not so much as turn on the Democratic Convention even once. I rented a Janis Joplin concert video instead. She is the finest in antidotal truth serum.

Way Over Yonder

I'm not a chump to social pressure anymore. The last time I was on that bender I bought a house. If that's what society wants from me, society is an idiot.

And so were we. I remember telling the realtor that I didn't know quite how to articulate it, but this dismal grid of houses we were looking at didn't feel like a neighborhood. Maybe if the road curved a little bit. Something, anything. The realtor snapped at me, "This area is purely residential!" and that settled that. She then quickly rhapsodized, "When the closing is over, you just can't wait to spend the first night in your new home."

During the gray blur that was the house-hunting phase, my husband would stare at cable TV late into the night, saying things like, "Any house is the same as any other. I feel nothing when I see a house." To compensate, I remember getting wildly giddy about the whole thing, sketching the floor plan of our randomly-selected dream house for anyone and everyone. I pointed out all the amazing features, like a hallway and a staircase, of the house we just had to have or I'd be driven to despair.

Be careful what you wish for.

After the closing, I discovered that this floor plan of mine was a fantasy, representing a bizarre composite of all eight houses we had seen ever so briefly. Our reality-based dwelling had no hallway at all. It did have a staircase, but part of its turn-of-the-twentieth-century charm was a narrowness which would not tolerate the dimensions of a mattress. And thus we began sleeping in the room off the kitchen, facing the neighbor's house five feet away, which offered a view of their mattress, which they had discarded and propped up against the outside of their house for safekeeping.

For two years we watched with no interest while that mattress withstood wind, rain, sleet, and snow. Its owners, however, were not as impressive, to make a very ugly story exceedingly short. I believe police reports are public record, if you require any further information.

Looking back, the best indicator that we had made a big mistake was our apparent refusal to move into the house after the closing. When we got back to our apartment that afternoon, I called everyone in my family to tell them we had just bought a house, and everybody said they couldn't wait to see it and they'd come right over that night. I said, "Okay, but can somebody pick us up?"

My brother drove us over to our house, where everyone we knew was lined up along the curb. They came from far and wide, the old and the young, and my brother popped champagne corks and produced crystal glasses and, after the trumped-up tour, we all sat on the floor of the empty house and had a wonderful time until the wee hours. Then, one by one, they drifted away, with parting congratulations, into the night until only my brother remained and I said, "Do you think you could maybe drive us home?" and he drove us back across town to our third-floor efficiency apartment, where we stayed for two more weeks.

Finally, we felt too guilty to put off moving any longer. The realtor had insisted that no new homeowners can keep away from their dream house, come hell or high water, so we were feeling like something must be wrong with us. We were failing society and, worse yet, we were failing our realtor.

But there was no way to get from our apartment to our house without a car, which we had been told not to buy until after the closing because the mortgage application would look a lot better without a car loan. That had seemed sensible, except then all our money was surreptitiously nibbled up by closing costs.

So, with one eye on the rising social barometer, we cash-advanced a down payment on a car. Yes indeed, the day had come when we were fresh out of excuses. We stuffed our belongings into this big old car we couldn't afford and, checking the map, drove past bars with names like The Poodle (breakfast served at 8 a.m.) to find the home in which we yearned to nest, or so we were told.

The next morning we awoke to find our new car stolen. We were stranded again. But at least we were in our new house, present and accounted for. And that would surely satisfy our realtor, a ruthless profiteer who had oddly, and perhaps arbitrarily, replaced society as proprietor of the approval we so perfunctorily sought.

It's worth noting that, shortly after the closing, our realtor contracted a long and inconvenient ailment. I may be immune to social pressure these days, but I've developed quite a fascination with karma.

A Concrete Image

Okay, so our steps exploded the first month we lived in our new house and we climbed a chunky sandpile to our back door for six months and everybody hates us. So what.

But the pressure, the pressure. All winter, we kept telling the neighbors that every time we wanted to fix the steps there was another freeze and we couldn't pour concrete. Never mind that when we finally made new steps they were wood. And that they sat tipped over in the middle of the yard for three weeks while we pounded out the concrete chunks at our back door. Okay, my husband pounded concrete. He borrowed his mom's sledgehammer (he didn't see any humor in my question, "How does your mother have occasion to own a sledgehammer?"), and he somehow even got mud in his teeth. It was a sight to see. He was sweating and swearing like a man with a sledgehammer, wearing my fashion sunglasses as goggles.

But where on earth, literally, do you put the finished pile of crumbled concrete steps? The smallest crumble weighs about five pounds, and darned if we could load it into the car. The sand from it had already killed half our foot-long grass, so now we had a patch of yellow thatching to deal with under the concrete. We left the pile there, intent on thinking it over for a few weeks. Except we came home two nights ago and neighbor kids had obviously been playing on it, which is an attractive nuisance lawsuit made in heaven. It was strewn all over the yard.

The pressure, the pressure. My husband's idea was that

any activity that involved his lifting a piece of concrete and moving in some recognized compass direction was obvious progress. I was of the opinion that we shouldn't move it at all until we know what's going to happen to it, because we might be wasting our (his) sweaty, swearing energy. So he heaved concrete over by the garage and wrecked up his finger and I made shot-in-the-dark phone calls in the cool house, sipping coffee. Each was convinced the other was doing absolutely nothing meaningful to solve the problem.

So while he grunted and grew to resent me more and more, I tried to think like my dad. I called the Construction Worker's Local 369. I think I got somebody's high school daughter on the line, and she said she had never heard of recycling concrete at construction sites. So I asked her what she personally would do in this situation. She said she'd ask the garbage collector to make a special trip. Now, I'd already tried the garbage department phone number a dozen times, and I kept trying to imagine just who was on the phone with them so much and how many lines they had and how many people had pounded out steps this week. Finally, I got through, and they seemed to think this was a reasonable question, and they referred me to somebody who could refer me to somebody. So I called the second number, and they answered something like "MRI," which I thought was a body scanning device, and they referred me to another place, where somebody else's little daughter got the phone and said she'd get Steve, which sounded like a good idea.

Steve said to box it up in lifting-weight (read: weight-lifting) boxes and that the price could be anywhere from $45 on up. Up to what, I may never know. You see, Steve just can't tell without looking at it, and he'd sure hate to misquote the price. So I went out to tell my husband that all our problems had been solved, but the concrete he was hefting had to be in boxes. Seething, in an endearing sort of way, he announced that concrete falls right through a box and that the hauler will just have to deal with the pile of pieces when they get here. I said they're going to turn around and leave if they see that, and he turned around and left.

I returned to the cool house to call Steve back and tell him that the boxes bottom out and we just can't do that, but that we'd be willing to help load, whatever we have to do, and he said, "You must be on vacation." I'm still puzzling over that one, because he's the one who said we had to be home. Maybe a working person could be home, but only a vacationing person would help load. I don't know. So Steve said they'd be there on a chosen day anytime after 12. I chose to believe him.

In the meantime, to make a good showing, I started bringing the pieces I could lift over to the garage, too, figuring if I could sweat and swear enough, I could make up for my can't-get-myself-to-hide-it air of superiority over placing the problem-solving phone call. My husband kept trying to tell me that I sure had done a lot of work, but why don't I quit for now, which means that my ridiculous pile of tiny pieces is only going to annoy Steve, and he'll either leave them there or charge us a fortune to gather them up. But I said, playing up my pathetic scheme to put in an honest, however pointless, day's work, "No, no, that's okay. You go rest up, and I'll just keep hauling these," which I did for about three minutes, until it started to rain and we decided to leave it at that until the big hauling day. Maybe it would mulch.

So here we are on Hauling Day, reunited in spirit and aim, as the sun is sinking toward the horizon, gazing fondly toward a big pile of big cement chunks and a little pile of little cement chunks, and, like the iceman, "I just know he's not going to come."

CLEANLINESS IS NEXT TO IMPOSSIBLE

I've decided that the key to spring cleaning and general household management is honesty, not diligence. Plan to repeat your mistakes in an orderly and predictable way, and you'll soon be enjoying the satisfaction of a well-run home. For instance, designate a special shelf in the refrigerator for food you want to spoil. This section should be reserved for restaurant doggie bags and cooking failures that you feel too guilty to throw out. Then, once a quarter, say, clean out the shelf, containers and all, without removing any protective wrapping. You know the food is rotten to the core by then, and it's much better to buy new storage dishes than to have to tie that dishtowel over your nose and mouth and run back and forth between the garbage and the toilet, that whole routine where you scoop out a little bit of that foamy yellow stuff that used to be potatoes with long barbecue tongs and then go throw up and then come back for another tongful, until the process is complete. Better to simply stock up on extra Tupperware.

It's good to have a crisp policy regarding coins that have fallen on the floor, which phenomenon appears to be the greatest hindrance to daily household maintenance. For me, the mere thought of picking up a penny or a nickel produces that heavy feeling you get as a kid in the fabric and pattern store. But I will always go for the dimes and quarters, because a few of them can approximate a can of Coke or a streetcorner phone call. My husband, on the other hand, will always pick up nickels but not dimes. He values weight over denomination (which is a good thing for me, should I become fat and broke).

The most relentless problem for many of us, if we're honest, is "little piles." If you claim that the impression of clutter your home conveys is really the result of an elaborate sorting process, let me clue you in that nobody's buyin' it.

We have a little pile of stuff just inside the front door designated "things that belong in the car": a comb, a pair of figure skates, proof of insurance. There's another little pile of stuff next to the phone for "things that require a phone call": our health club membership renewal that we don't want to call about yet because the club might go under (the free towels keep getting smaller and smaller), an ad for a restaurant in Chicago where we might want to make reservations if we should someday get a craving for a Type A weekend trip, an invitation to a wedding in France that's waiting for me to conquer my fear of planes and waiting for both of us to suddenly become . . . I believe the word is "solvent."

My brother-in-law calls us the reigning king and queen of "little piles." When company comes over, we typically launch into our fervent explanation that these piles are actually highly evolved, but lately the guests have begun to exchange knowing glances, the kind that tell you they talked about our little piles on the way over in the car.

This morning we decided to do something about our reputation, doggone it. We stood in the middle of the living room, surveying things from a safe distance until our eyes glazed over. Then suddenly my husband snapped out of that chorebound daze and briskly suggested, "Okay, first let's make a little pile of all the things we want to throw out."

I recently marched off to the store and bought a green breadbox and stuffed it with every urgent little scrap of paper from all over the house and tied it tightly shut with a pretty blue ribbon. There.

6. THREE DEGREES
OF GENERATIONS

HOW OLD WAS MOTHER EARTH
WHEN SHE EARNED HER TITLE?

At a party last week, not 48 hours after my birthday, a new acquaintance of about three minutes asked how old I was. Still in birthday girl spirit, I announced, "I just turned 44." She said, "Do you have children?" I said, "No." She said, and I quote, "Are you selfish, or what?"

Yow. "What the hell is it your business?" came to mind, but not fast enough. I was totally knocked off balance. Instead, I chirped rather hysterically, "We're broke!" The woman chattered on, but I wasn't really listening. My mind was buzzing with: "What would possess me to chirp, 'We're broke!'?"

As soon as I saw my opportunity, I made a break for it. Scarcely moments into my escape, I plunged headlong into the time-honored pastime of thinking up too-late-but-darn-near-showstopping comebacks. Next time, I was going to be ready.

Because that was the point, right? The only problem was my lame comeback. Right?

Okay, wrong. I admit it, this oblivious woman struck a nerve I didn't even know I had. But, I mean, good heavens, there are a million very personal reasons why a woman of 44 whole years wouldn't have children....Okay, maybe none of them applies to me, but there's also the good reason that I don't have to have a good reason if I don't feel like it. So there. I am, of course, folding my arms defiantly at this point.

If I did have any reasons, though—and no one's saying I do—these might be some of them: I want to iron out all of my neuroses first, so I don't pass them on. I'd like to have even $20 saved first. I'm not sure I'm strong enough to carry the squirming equivalent of a sack of hot flour all day on four hours' sleep. I fret mercilessly about how to swing the health insurance costs and about my weak first aid skills. And, to save the most scandalous for last, my husband and I are having too much fun alone together, and we're not ready to share. Wait, back up, there it is. Did you hear that? "Not ready to share." She's right. Selfish. Wow. Who knew?

I guess, if I had to say, which I don't, the right time for me to have children is when I can't stand to wait one more day—for six months straight. Not that I haven't been tempted away from this half-baked policy. My brother and his wife were recently shocked awake at 5 AM by their little bitty fella requesting an "ice told Tote." And sure, when I heard that story I thought, I gotta get some of that for myself. Coke, I mean. Just kidding. Or am I? And around it goes. That's why I'm saying six unequivocating months straight. Because this is really, really serious stuff.

In the meantime, I have finally hit on the right answer to that unseemly woman's question. It's a classic case of I-can't-believe-I-didn't-think-of-this-before inspiration. If

some jelly-mouthed worm says, "Are you selfish, or what?'
the correct choice, clearly, is "What."

There Oughta Be a Law

Whenever I see that Statue of Liberty billboard saying,
"Is it possible she has no maternal instincts?" I take it per-
sonally. It's kind of a community wisdom in our family that
I only babysit under heavy adult supervision.

Like there was the time my sister-in-law was beastly sick
and called me at six in the morning to come over and see
about my nephew, who was at the early crawling stages.
All I had to do was sit two feet from the ailing parent and
keep the child occupied until more suitable help (like the
neighbor's beagle) could arrive.

Then the unthinkable happened. He voiced an alarming
interest in nourishment. So I donned my surgeon's mask (I
know that much) and feverishly dumped some white powder in a bottle and added either water or milk, I forget, and
shook it up. Using hot dog tongs, I held the top under boiling water for ten minutes.

Then I scuttled the sweaty baby and foaming bottle back
to his mother's side, where we both felt safer, and balanced
him and the bottle on the floor. But the baby just tipped over
in slow motion and whimpered listlessly on all fours. All
that fuss about being hungry, and now all he would do was
chew idly at that rubber thing on the top. Trying to sound
mellow for his mother's benefit, I cooed, "Now, I don't think

we chew the bottle so much as drink from it, right, honey?" Then I heard the faint strains of my sister-in-law's halting response, "I...think...maybe if you...hold it." Now, see, how was I supposed to know that he couldn't pick up a bottle?

I came back a year later, because a quitter never wins. I marched over to the baby and set a hot dog in front of him. Just because I could. But all he did was roll it around. So I said, "I don't think we quite roll the hot dog around so much as eat it, right, honey?" Mom said, "I think maybe if you cut it up into small pieces." Okay. I diced it into confetti and he was heading for it when Mom said, "I think maybe if you take the skin off. A hot dog skin is like a balloon." I suppose a comment like that means something to the maternally instinctive. So I peeled the skins off 150 little slippery pieces of hot dog, knowing that I'd have nightmares that I missed one.

I was relieved when we got to the banana course, because I heard tell he takes those whole. So I placed a banana in front of him, rather triumphantly, I might add. But all he did was rock it back and forth. So I said, "I don't think we quite rock the banana back and forth so much as eat it, right, honey?" And Mom said, "I think maybe if you were to peel the banana."

If history is the best predictor of the future, I'm in trouble. Aren't I under some obligation to inform the proper authorities of this deficit in my mental processes? Shouldn't it be on my driver's license or something? When my nephew turns three, I think I'll just give him cabfare to Murray's (home of the butterknife steak) for dinner. It's for the best.

THE INFANCY OF NOMENCLATURE

I suffer from an unusual condition: I can't stop thinking up names for babies.

And there's one more thing. They're all undesirable. At least, that's what everyone says who has participated in the informal polling process.

Fortunately, I have a potentially infinite amount of time in which to refine my choices, seeing as how there are no babies in our house (although I recently asked my hair stylist why my hair was suddenly curly and she asked if I'd had a baby and I said no and she said, "Are you sure?").

At least I understand that every name for a baby has to have a pleasant and natural nickname built in. You can't give a baby a name meant for a retired lawyer, I don't care what your hyperaspirations are for the child.

Here are the hapless results of this week's brainstorming:

For a girl:

Bovine (Vinny)
Beluga (Lugie)
Deliria (Lira)
Serotonin (Rotini)
Plasma (Ma)
Nutmeg (Nut)
Malicia (CIA)
Chutney (Utne)
Placenta (Penny)

Don't ask me where the emphasis on large mammals—both aquatic and grazing—and vital fluids originated.

For a boy:

Tuxedo (Tux)
Askance (Skan)
Gymnasium (Gym)
Op-Ed (Opie)
Plankton (Anklet)
Tavist-D (Taffy)

My husband is convinced a boy named Tuxedo would get beaten up in the locker room. Actually, that's the test by which he measures the potential of every boy's name. So far it's a massacre.

I wonder if there's some form of aversive therapy I could apply to my little problem. Maybe they could wire me up so that every time a name lurches untimely into my consciousness I am forced to eat feta cheese.

THE IDEAL MOTHER'S DAY GIFT IS AN EAR

Put down that perfume! I have come up with the perfect Mother's Day present.

I know how you can make your mother's wildest dreams come true, no matter who your mother is or how old she is or how old you are. And it won't cost you a cent. You might even profit.

As Mother's Day is dawning, you appear before your mother and speak these words: "Mom, I want this Mother's Day to be the happiest day of your entire life. My gift to you does not come in a box with a card. I am not going to make you breakfast."

You're going to have to bite the bullet to deliver the punchline: "Today, for this single day in all of eternity, I am going to follow your advice. All of it."

Now, some of you may be excused at this point because those words have already made your mom dizzy with delight. You can go back home, back to bed, taking full credit for a job well done. And don't forget to save that standby perfume for next year.

The rest of you may not be so lucky. Your mother's instructions may already be flying out of her mouth so fast that your hair is wafting behind you like a model's. Which brings us to the extremely obvious first phase of this torturer/tortured arrangement: your hair. Your awful, too-long or too-damaged or just plain too-ugly hair that she's been dying to get her hands on for, well, decades. And it's Sunday and the stylists are all home with their mothers, so you know what that means. The bathroom and the scissors and quite possibly a curling iron, with the main goal being to get the hair out of your eyes "so everyone can see your beautiful face."

The butchering completed, the next step is undoubtedly your shoes. As my husband's mother said to him in a stage whisper the minute she met me, "Here's $50. Not the shoes with the holes with the nice girl." Now, we've all been given shoe money countless times before and we've always spent it on records and movies and beer. And perhaps your mom has always been like Charlie Brown with the football and tried it again. So it's been a good, long run, but it's over. Because this time you have to buy the shoes. It's part of the deal.

Now that your mom's addressed the head and the feet, there's that whole region in between. Basically, say goodbye to those comfy second-hand clothes. Sons, say hello to white Penguin tennis shirts and tan wide-wale (what is that?) corduroys with Coach belts (and don't worry, your mom will not need prompting to tell you what to do with that leather Coach tag that looks too expensive to cut off but also looks like something only an idiot would leave on; she's been itching to advise you on such matters).

Daughters, say hello to floral print dresses with puffy sleeves and dainty waists from which you need the jaws of life to free yourself at the end of the painful day. It may surprise you—then again, it probably won't—that your mom has had this clothing boxed and ready in her closet for years, just in case you should ever take leave of your senses and do exactly what you've done today: hand her the reins.

Now there's the small matter of your personality. Change it, your mom will tell you. Learn to take criticism. Snap out of that naïve radical politics phase you're in; it only makes people avoid you. Don't interrupt. Get rid of those low-class friends you've clearly outgrown; they're impeding your natural ambition. Dress like a professional and you'll be treated like one. "A professional what?" you might ask.

That's another thing, your mother will announce. Sarcasm is unattractive. It turns people off. You'll never get married if you don't learn to smile all the time. And make eye contact. You can't expect everything to come to you with no effort. Get up earlier. There is no reason a healthy young person like you can't be up at 7 every morning. You need to get with the schedule the rest of the world is on.

Your mom will have a lot more to say about the ineffectual impression you're making on the world, but you will have stopped listening somewhere back during that comment about taking criticism. That's OK. At this stage, just let the freight train roll. The fine—and gross—tuning of your disappointing existence will continue late into the evening.

But you won't care because today, as God is your witness, you've really done it. You are going to fall asleep without so much as a molecule of guilt in your body for the first time since the day you were born. And for that you have your mom to thank, because only the person who brought you into this world has the power to take away your guilt.

You hear yourself murmuring "Happy Mother's Day" as you smile yourself into dreamland in your crispy new striped pajamas.

GRANDMA'S HEIRLOOM

I've never seen a woman with so many silk dresses and china cups as my grandma. She's 95 years old—well, okay, 94. You always stretch it a little when they near that age. It's more dramatic, and the president writes longer letters commemorating her historic existence. But the time has come for her to move to a nursing home, at least for a while, until she recovers from a fall that resulted from the excitement of hearing the phone ring, even though she was waiting for the call. So we all packed off to her little house in West Fargo and helped her sort through her treasures and move out of her place.

We had developed four piles: throw out, move to a local storage facility for the time being, send back to Minneapolis to adorn the Grandma Room of my parents' house, and bring to the nursing home. These, of course, are listed in order of ascending honor.

Here's how she ruled. Collector plates with deer on them: Grandma Room in Minneapolis. China: garbage. Figurines: garbage. Crocheted snowflakes: storage until Christmas. Pictures of grandchildren: Grandma Room. Pictures of great-grandchildren: nursing home. Expensive gifts from my mother over the last 50 years: garbage.

Get the basic idea? Okay. We're getting to the rubble part of the day, the part that never ends, the part where the men are suddenly charged with a desire to lift heavy boxes and call utility companies, and the daughters and granddaughters pick up one object after another endless little object and wait for its individual banishment.

Right when we figure we're getting the hang of it and we're barely pausing each thing in front of Grandma's face on its swing toward the garbage, we find out once and for all there's no accounting for taste. I pick up some rock and say, "Grandma, you don't want this, do you?" and she lights up like a Christmas tree and says, "What do you think it is?" and I say, "A rock, I don't know," and she has us pass it around and we all agree it's a rock. Now she's percolating with amusement. It appears that we have been passing around a petrified hairball straight from a cow's stomach, compliments of her alcoholic butcher friend.

This after my mother has informed the nursing home that Grandma needs sensitive care as she is a creative genius who is used to the finer things and needs silk and lace to be everywhere apparent. I don't know why my mother said all that, but I've never put a 95-year-old woman into a nursing home. Regardless, the stage has been set for her delicate arrival and won't they be surprised.

Hairball: nursing home.

7. Oh, Say Can I See (And Other Holiday Hootenannies)

The Meat Mystique

The Fourth of July means only one thing to the American male: raw meat. Forget fireworks, flags, family, even potato salad. These elements only serve as accessories to the main event: the tray of raw meat.

The oohs and aahs issuing forth from the guests gathered around the grill far exceed any to be elicited by the spectacular fireworks display the sated group will later attend. The pride a child feels while wielding a sparkler cannot touch the self-satisfaction of the "chef" as the meat hits the grill and the first sizzle is heard.

It is further lost on this horde that the myriad women bearing covered dishes—each dish reflecting days of meticulous preparation—might more appropriately be called "chef." The women's 12-tiered tortes simply cannot compete with 16 ounces of bleeding bovine flesh. No, their tortes and other delicate creations are regarded merely as condiments, much as mustard, to enhance the grilled wonder.

If I understand the procedure correctly, you drop the meat onto the grill with a long fork. After awhile, you spear the meat with the long fork and flip it over. Lather, rinse, repeat, basically. Then the cooked meat is speared yet again and dropped onto a platter or onto the paper plate of the next in line. Miracle complete.

So, I am forced to ask, what is the big deal? Is it that raw meat is the only food the guests, who are kept outdoors, can see and therefore believe is truly theirs to eat? Is it the chef's apron, replete with a clever saying like "Don't bother the cook" that elevates his status? Or the utterly unnecessary oven mitts that perhaps remind one of boxing and by association raise the perceived testosterone level of the fork-holder?

Could it be too much beer?

Maybe it's all about fire. The ritual begins with a bag of coals. There is much heated discussion about the most efficient and artful way to arrange the briquettes. This turns out to be your basic pile. The coals are then doused, way beyond the recommended dosage, with lighter fluid. The match is lit. The flames erupt. They—the blaze and the men—simmer down to half an hour of glowing and smoking until the Moment of Raw Meat, when the flames rally and burst forth in enthusiastic response to the spray of animal fluids and A-1 sauce.

Perhaps the mystical cookout is simply an expression of the male preoccupation with the power of fire, a fascination summoned forth by a primal survival instinct. That theory strikes me as more plausible, and far more accessible to the logical mind, than the notion that grilling meat is even a skill, much less an act worthy of unbridled admiration.

So, then, men grill in order to survive. In order that we all may survive. And for that I am grateful.

Brawn on the Fourth of July

Oh, to be in Canada, a contiguous beacon in the pitch dark of the American conscience. But I'm broke, and I'm stuck here.

Twenty-four glorious hours of blowing on my stars and stripes plastic pinwheel and waving my gold-polyester-fringed flag with the missile superimposed on the front. Yessirree, this is going to be a hootenanny. Maybe I'll make star-shaped cookies and sprinkle those little silver candy BBs all over them. Or shave little star-shaped paths onto my scalp. The possibilities twinkle before me on this proud and long-awaited holiday, like a thousand shards of napalm.

I jump every time a neighbor kid's bottle rocket goes off. Now little boys igniting fireworks strike me as sinister. No matter how much I blink, I keep seeing them in uniform. All I see are tiny little future recruits for the next big bully fireworks we pull on a tiny little unsuspecting country that has something we want. And, in the nick of time, our governor just cut pre-school funding. Thank goodness pre-military-toy toddlers won't be subject to that pesky creative coopera-tion thing nursery school is so famous for.

How am I going to survive the Fourth of July? Especially knowing that New York just put on its biggest, most ex-pensive parade in history to tastefully purr (remember, Bush said we don't want to gloat) over our aggression. This isn't about being glad soldiers made it home alive. It's about get-ting primed to send them to another corner of the earth with bigger weapons next time. It's "Look out, world, we're just warming up here." All in the name of patriotism.

Flags are being used as weapons to shut me up, but it isn't working. Flags are just blueprints for cheap trash trinkets, which are sold in the name of pride but are meant to line the pockets of convenience store suppliers. But, hey, that's what America's all about. Making a buck, any way you can. Explain to me how it honors "the troops" (whose status as diverse people has dissolved) or the flag if I sweat in a bikini with a starred top and striped bottoms. I don't get it.

Can't we pick this day of all days to say enough is enough? Doesn't anybody feel queasy yet? Shall we stage a slide show of our next (long-since planned) bomb targets to fuel the hype? Shall we tip over a truck? Grunt and burp? I think I heard Bush say, "We've chosen utter loss of decorum as our special way of saying thanks. Thanks for grinding your heel on an anthill."

I say let's deflate our chests a few inches. Let some air out of our heads and our balloons and see if we don't feel a little healthier.

BURNING THE YULE LOG AT BOTH ENDS

Everyone in our family wants to spend Christmas Eve at our parents' house, and generally offers to spend all of Christmas Day at their in-laws'. Except everyone's spouse makes the exact same offer, not at all fooled by that old Christmas Day ruse. Christmas Eve is everyone's favorite.

So what to do? My mom always says, "Honey, you do

whatever you want. But just let me tell you who's going to be here, and what I'm making for dinner." And she talks softly about the fireplace and the presents and the tree, and my eyes well up. She can put together a Christmas that would make Currier & Ives want to hang it up.

There has got to be a solution. Okay, there's spending part of Christmas Eve at each place. That puts you on the freeway, passing a lot of other irritable couples, at about eight o'clock Christmas Eve. My family is just sitting down to dinner, and I barely get to see them, when we have to leave for *his* parents' house. A long ride to the other side of the earth, and we arrive just in time for my husband's family to get up from the table, overfed and ready for a nap. We pick at the leftovers. Everyone has fun but us.

Another year we admitted we were scared to grow up yet. We each went off to our own parents' house for Christmas Eve. We even stayed over like when we were little. And spent most of the time on the phone with each other, shivering in the basement (the only place you can hear above the madding crowd), crabby and hopelessly lonesome. We agreed that we were really expecting a lot from everyone to make up for our sacrifice. We kept thinking, "I don't know, that joke wasn't that funny," and "This fireside coffee isn't all it's cracked up to be," and generally wondering how we ever thought this could be a good idea.

So we press on to the third option, each sacrificing Christmas Eve to the other on alternating years. And one of us will feel guilty and follow the other one around, saying, "Are you sure this is okay?" And the other one, entirely sure it's not okay, and just short of tears, will say, "It's fine. I'm having fun." But you try to tell yourself, next year, next year it's at my parents'. Then you realize, as they say in *Alice in Wonderland*, you get Christmas Eve every other year—and this isn't any other year.

Then you figure, maybe we should have both families over to our house and solve the whole problem. Except that my parents have the 13-foot Christmas tree, and my brother has flatly informed me that he won't come to my house because I can't compete with that. And Grandma and the babies are all settled in and comfortable at my parents', and my husband's sister sings in her choir in the middle of the whole mess anyway, and it's all hopeless to coordinate, and whatever happened to childlike wonder and all of that?

It's hard for everyone. The other night I'm sitting at the end of my parents' bed, the meeting place of the house, and Mom is at her wits' end, trying to devise a plan—or algorithm, as it evolved—to house all the guests in a limited number of rooms and beds. She was getting that Christmas headache voice that steals over each of us at some point, and I piped up out of the blue, "Shall we all remember what Christmas is all about?" and she started to laugh, and she laughed until I laughed, and we laughed until I hiccupped and had to go swallow seven sips of water while holding my breath, and on the seventh sip I realized that this was one of those Christmas moments, and I need look no further.

'TIS THE SEASON: IF YOU LIE LIKE A RUG, I'LL SING LIKE A BIRD

It's a money-back guarantee that at any given point over the course of the holidays your somehow multiplying house-guests will bark out each of dozens of erroneous clichés. If you want to be the annoying one in the group (and, really, must there be just one?), you can take the culprit to task over the actual empirical significance of the kneejerk utter-ance. It's an indirect but altogether satisfying way of getting back at people for squeezing the toothpaste from the middle and drinking out of the Beep carton. Ready?

If your Uncle Vinny booms out that he "slept like a baby" last night, he is doubtless feeling mighty peaked today. After all, he woke up every two hours crying.

If that Cousin Meredith of yours really "eats like a bird," then she must, by my calculations, consume the rough equiv-alent of 1,440 McDonald's quarter pounders per day (okay, assuming you hold the bun) to reach the requisite 300% of her weight. Let's hope you receive a bulk discount or you're going to have to start sending her to bed without supper when the rations dry up, I don't care if it is Christmas Eve.

And if you believe your Cousin Jasper that his new Trans Am "runs like a top," then chances are you just saw it from the kitchen window, spiraling out of control all the way down the icy driveway in a blur, until a tree took mercy on it and you quick jerked the curtains shut to preserve the fragile Christmas spirit.

If your Grandma Esther exclaims how the new housedress you just gave her "fits like a glove," take it back, 'cause you know that she had to use her teeth to pull on the second sleeve, and furthermore it's making her sweat and inhibiting her finer motor skills.

If you asked your little granddaughter Marcy to "quick like a bunny" go get the paper towels, don't expect her back before the stain sets indelibly because, unless those pet store bunnies are really depressed (which is entirely possible) and therefore a wholly unreliable sample, it seems to me that a rabbit's eyes tend toward the drooping, right along with its ears and its sinking body in general, and it's got that perpetual gimme-one-good-reason look.

If you tell your little brother Marty he's "growing like a weed," by all means keep the path clear, because he might be storming past you any second. After all, consider his destiny on the basis of your observation. The growth of a weed is watched with frank disgust and horror, while visions of its thorough and speedy destruction dance violently in your head. And you thought teenagers were just touchy.

(I can't help but offer several of the outtakes that insistently crowded my brain well into the night during the creation of this essay, quite to the exclusion of the bona fide examples I sought: burp like an urchin, moan like a cactus, snip like a goat, and—my personal favorite—barf like an elf. If spoken with the proper authority, these could start a trend.)

BE ON THE GIVING END OF HOLIDAY MAYHEM

For the most part, holiday gatherings are a bleary montage of throbbing smiles and uncomfortable, improbable clothes. The paradoxical phrase "ill at ease" takes on new meaning as we become more shrill and bloated with each passing celebration.

But have cheer: It is possible to boobytrap the formal atmosphere and experience comic relief first-hand in the process. The key is to covertly challenge others' knowledge of and adherence to gracious protocol:

Serve oily little olives with pits in them, then sit back and take in the action. Do people try to deposit the pit onto that curly appetizer fork and lower it precariously to the plate? Do they expel the pit into a cocktail napkin, almost as though laying an egg, then tuck the napkin into a crack in the couch or a neighbor's blazer pocket? Is there a great-uncle who would actually swallow it, only to spend the next two weeks checking ears and nostrils for budding olive branches?

Sure, there are obvious etiquette traps, like mistletoe and fingerbowls and four forks arranged in ascending size, but the idea is to be more subtle than that. Think up things the guests haven't hammered out in the car on their way over. Try leaving the soap in the shower, not in the sinkside soapdish. Granted, you can't witness the percentage of guests who will duck behind the shower curtain to lather up, but you'll know each and every guest is sweating out the decision at some point in the evening.

Serve the traditional Christmas goose, but with a particularly sticky glaze, and provide only the finest Danish appliquéd cloth napkins. Then spend half the meal dreamily recounting to your guests the day you uncovered these precious linens in a cozy, snowy little town on your only trip to Europe.

This is all in good fun, you understand. And fun you shall have.

The next lesson in imperceptible mischief concerns gift-giving. Again, avoid the obvious, such as too much concealed tape or box within box within box. Instead, consider writing a clear "TO" name on a gift tag, but make the "FROM" illegible. The gift in question should be expensive and confoundingly personal. Perhaps a fuzzy photograph in a sterling frame.

Similarly, toy with the duplicate-present phenomenon. (Invariably, two different aunts end up buying a common nephew the same thing—usually the game Operation. He is forced to blather on about their uncanny intuition because it's still his favorite game and how did they still know, etc., etc.) This year, take the offensive. Here's the plan: Give your cousin the same gift twice in one evening. Both unmistakably from you. Same wrapping, same card, same everything. Choose something no one could reasonably need two of, like an informational video about Select Comfort mattresses (or even one of, like a garlic roaster). Offer no explanation, just two big, eager hope-you-like-it smiles.

All the while, have a bass-heavy rap album playing in the background, but too softly to warrant an objection from the larger-than-you-remembered conservative faction. (They're the ones who hog—no offense to pigs—all the chairs and leave you sitting on the floor, leaning against the ottoman in your itchy little plaid skirt, from which vantage point you can hear but not see their coffee cup shakily hit the saucer directly over your head.)

Take heart, hale merrymakers. If you follow this simple recipe, visions of sugarplums will dance in your eyes throughout the festive marathon. By New Year's, though, you'll still feel like you've been run over by a speeding delivery truck. After all, there is a limit of one miracle per holiday season.

SOMEDAY MY FROG WILL COME

And you thought New Year's Eve was pressure. Valentine's Day looms large, and the have-nots may as well be wearing a sandwich board announcing their unflagging undesirability.

It takes only a cursory review of one's sordid personal history to chronicle a lifetime of pathetic rejection on Valentine's Day. It starts early. Consider first grade, when you actively participate in your own ultimate humiliation by constructing a shoe box with a slit in the top and heart-shaped doilies stuck all over it. Then, the next day, your one friend Butch drops a Valentine in your shoe box and everyone can hear it land with a thud.

In the meantime, you're marching up and down the

rows, rather anonymously depositing a Valentine into all 32 kids' boxes because your mom told you it wasn't nice to leave anyone out. She apparently was not moved to share that philosophy with the other mothers. So, anyway, Butch's box is crammed full, so much so that Nadine-Elaine Thurwell actually has to tap hers into his box. The thing is, you know Butch jammed an entire Woolworth's Valentine's Day assortment pack into his shoebox when no one was looking at him, which was all the time.

Although the psychic damage is, of course, permanent, the shoebox phase does pass. But it is replaced in high school by something still more odious: Carnation Day. Carnation Day consists of nasty little people filling out mean little cards that are attached to insipid pink carnations and delivered to homeroom in a garishly long, drawn-out pageant. When it's all over, the popular kids wield veritable bouquets and you and Butch sit there smelling the grit of the desk cleaner, thinking surly thoughts about how carnations are so middle-class anyway.

This is a brutal experience. And it doesn't even help to know that the already-superpopular Carlene Harris ordered those six carnations for herself, with six forged cards, and then insisted on keeping them in her locker in stead of carrying them "so other people who didn't get any won't feel bad."

Carnation Day does eventually fade into a pulsing nightmare, while the ensuing college years positively throb with promise. You feel opportunity in the air, around every corner. Sure, your model/cheerleader roommate Tibsy gets three dozen sweetheart roses and a five-pound box of Godiva chocolates, the latter of which she sickly sweetly goads you to consume because she's on a diet and God—and everyone else—knows you're not. But you comfort yourself that Tibsy knows nothing of the meaning of life.

Senior year, Tibsy gets a diamond ring for Valentine's Day, hidden in a pink marzipan cake. That's the low point. It's clear sailing from there. Your adult friends are above this foolishness. Sure, all those about you are entwining and spawning cherubic offspring, but that's about them, after all, not about you.

Until the phone call comes. It's Butch. You haven't heard from him in ten years. He wants you to know if you can babysit for the twins so that he and Carlene can fly to New York for a romantic candlelit dinner at Tavern on the Green, where violins may potentially be present, on Valentine's Day. It all happens so fast. Somehow, there you are, left with a pediatrician's phone number and free access to mixed nuts because the regular babysitter, Tibsy's little 14-year-old bombshell sister, has a hot date. And, doubtless, a gaggle of carnations she must attend to.

The only relief comes from the peaceful knowledge that each phase of degradation is never the last; the torment is self-renewing. And you wander around Butch's living room in the bright red velvet dress you wore just in case, narrowing your eyes at wedding pictures between shrill a capella verses of "Someday My Prince Will Come," while one three-year-old hisses at the other through the banister, "Who's that big red lady?"

8. Taxes R Us

Inscrutable Scribbles
Hold the Key to Crucial Tax Deductions

I've been working obsessively on our taxes for days on end, and a startling phenomenon has arisen in the process. Every time I sift through a new scoop of receipts from the tax drawer, I find another little scribbled note that makes no sense. I'm sure these notes served a vital purpose when written, but I strongly suspect it's too late now to recoup their financial usefulness. Check these:

Sears Brand Central??
No. Babies will not eat dog food on my shift.

Each enigmatic message holds the key to a crucial tax deduction. But so far I've rattled these keys in every lock I can think of and no doors have swung open to yield a cascade of gold coins. There is, after all, such a thing as an audit, and I almost feel as if these scraps of paper form a funnel through which I will swirl directly into the low chair opposite the imposing desk of the assigned Internal Revenue Service power broker. The IRS has never much cared for those of us whose "home office" is not a tower in the fastest-growing suburb but instead the narrow strip of carpet next to the bed. (You know, that dedicated square footage where the "reference books" and "appropriate office attire" pile up.)

It doesn't help to have supporting documentation like this, written on the backs of gum wrappers and unopened bills:

I am going to write poetry.
When you're stressed out, the first thing that goes is
recycling.

One layoff due to a Caterpillar strike (shear operator).

And after that last morsel, the odds became so highly stacked against me that I could no longer see the tax forms (which was fine with me, by then). The whole wad of pathetically inscrutable messages was poised over the trash bin when suddenly a critical phrase flashed in neon on my brain: "To the best of my knowledge...." So please, Your Majesty, consider the following tax-deductible, uh, informal receipts to be accounted for in a true and accurate manner, to the best of my knowledge:

Feet. Human feet. (houseguest)
3 machines
2 at a time
four in an hour
$50/hr.
Mature bulls attend individual cows rather than
maintain harems.

I hope this free financial advice has been of some inspiration to those of you still sweating out the tax forms while I get back to the matter of the mature bull, which reminds me that I clean forgot to write off my five visits to the State

Fair last year.

I'll have to file an amendment.

BIZARRE IRS FORM
DESERVES AN AUDIT WAY MORE THAN I DO

At this late date, I have stopped regarding my tax return as something that can be perfected. Now is just as good a time as any to sign my name on the line where you swear you didn't make stuff up.

Not that the IRS doesn't encourage flights of fancy with the options presented on their forms. I thought I had sat down well-prepared, with neat stacks of stapled, totaled receipts and every windowed envelope received in the month of January. Instead, as I began the process, I found myself rather ill-equipped for the disparate array of startling matters posed by the IRS for my consideration.

Right off the bat, they want to know if I'm a member of the clergy. I noted that I'd have to come back to that question because I've always wanted to be a deacon.

You are then required to review the sections of your Forms 1099, or nonemployee income. You know, the usual boxes: Rent, royalties, fishing boat proceeds....

First of all, how many faceless millions are out there on boats all day and night to warrant their very own box? Either they're a huge underworld, the true backbone of this country's commerce, or else some legislator spent months and months harping on a page 19 story about how some guy's uncle left his family $10,000 resulting from 50 years of quietly noodling for catfish every evening after work, and loophole chaos ensued. (Little did they know that noodling doesn't require a boat. So much wasted time.)

Now, about your EPP: This is Box 7 of the 1099. Apparently as common as the fishing boat entrepreneur is the early retiree who got too golden of a parachute. First of all, it appears that you need to be awarded three times your regular pay to even qualify for golden parachute status. The EPP stands for something like Excess Parachute Payment, meaning yes, there does exist too much of a good thing.

The instruction for calculating how much of your parachute (and you, unlike most of us, know what color yours is) constitutes excess reads something like: This is so complicated you'll need an accountant.

Later on in the form, you are asked to cast back and recall whether you have received a prize or award in 2007. You are further informed that you must return it before you spend it. Clear enough. Let's move on.

Have you received federal crop disaster payments? In my flight of fancy, this custom is expanded to all interested parties whose business endeavors are disastrous, as they so very often are. I would like to see a little something come my way the next time my widget goes south.

To save every possible penny, you are now asked to consider other income you might have, like "recovery of bad debt" (is there any other kind?), or, say, fuel tax credits or— the obvious cash cow—selling scrap. It's things like this we so often overlook.

Don't forget to take a deduction for ant oil, gas, other minerals, or timber—anything you can do that depletes natural resources is money in your pocket. Which brings me to advertising expenses: If you put your name on a bunch of junk, you get your money back. Pens, plastic bags (I believe you're depleting natural resources here, so remember those tricky indirect double-deductions), signs, display racks. What about tie racks, I'm left wondering.

Car expenses: Do you have a fleet of trucks? Again, don't be too hasty. It's worth taking a moment to check outside before you say no.

Among other things, goodwill (the quality, not the thrift shop) is considered an intangible property and can therefore be depreciated.

Deduct repair and maintenance of your property, sure, but forget about claiming aluminum siding. It ups the value so much that it doesn't qualify. The disparaging remarks about aluminum siding vendors, then, are as much sour grapes as the cracks about Kirby vacuum cleaner peddlers. These people are rich and their products are miracles. We all know it; let's shed the burdens of bitterness and jealousy as we close this tax season.

Remember that you have every right to deduct your legitimate home office; however, you will be audited beyond your worst nightmares, which already include furry fangs and a lot of golden-eyed drool.

A helpful hint to spare you hours of confusion: The "at-risk" rules must be applied before you apply the "passive activity" rules.

And now, under the None of Their Business category: Did you or your spouse take part in any like-kind exchanges during the past year? (What, like wife-swapping?)

They would also like to know if you've received any bartering income. What's the point of barter if you're going to report it? I suspect this issue refers back to the fishing boat proceeds and noodling and clergy—did you trade a catfish for an after-hours confession? Which party enjoyed the net profit?

I'm quite partial to this list of possible casualty and theft losses: by reason of hurricane, storm, flood, fire, burglary, or your investment counselor.

Remember to claim intangible drilling costs if you invest in oil, gas, and geothermal wells. (Are those the same as hot springs, the fountains of eternal youth? Are they for sale?)

Most importantly—I can't emphasize this enough—if you've amortized a pollution control facility, you must use the alternative depreciation system and the class life range using the straight line method.

God help you if you weren't paying attention just now. It would be a shame to mess up a perfectly good return with such a careless and avoidable error.

9. I Beg You're Pardoned

If You Have to Ask

It is becoming more and more apparent to me that most questions can be answered by "If you have to ask..."

Such as:

Do you think I should really marry Terry, or should I move to Mexico?

What would I do with myself all day if I weren't working?

I don't know, I think I'm pretty self-confident, don't you—or don't you?

If you're supposed to bake the cookies at 300 for 12 minutes, can't you just crank it up to 450 and do it for 8?

Was it something I said?

Hey, how long has that low fuel light been on?

Did you make that yourself? (And its corollary: Oh, did your kids make that?)

Are you within the sound of my voice?

Excuse me, did anybody see a wallet?

Are you home? Are you just standing there by the phone? Is anybody home? Hello? Are you there? Are you there? Are you there?

You're not one of them women's libbers, are you?

Am I interrupting?

Do you think it's possible, if you add all your credit cards together, and accept every new credit card offer, to amass a total credit limit that exceeds your annual income?

Do you think this mayonnaise has been in the sun too long?

What's this "NSF" supposed to mean?

Mom, what would you do if somebody made this, like, really cool mural of a sea otter on their wall and everything, except the coolest thing is it was made out of mint jelly, but the dog licked the flipper-tail off, would the dog get in big trouble?

Do you smell smoke?

So you think it was a bad idea to tell the interviewer I'm not one of those people who puts in twelve-hour days all the time like a maniac?

Honey, the kids are in the back seat with you, right?

Are those fangs detachable?

HUNGER FOR POETRY
LEAVES STOMACH IN THE LURCH

I've been trying really hard to get with the poetry scene because it's all the rage, but I guess I've picked the wrong spectator sport.

It's fair to say that I have seen over three dozen poetry performances in the last few months. I mean, I am really saturating myself, on the theory that with increased exposure will come a decrease in my inappropriate and involuntary merriment. For my own sake as well as that of the self-controlled patrons of these literary establishments, I have taken to sitting in the back. OK, way in the back. OK, on the floor next to the door so I can escape if I feel a chortle coming on.

Last night, determined to lick my restless amusement, I resisted the hunger-driven urge to head home at halftime and instead darted across the street for a roast beef and tomato sandwich to go. I slid back into home plate by the door just in time for this intense, black-clad poet to take the spotlight. It's a good thing I was squatting in the very back of a dark room to eat my sandwich, because those readings are so church-quiet that everyone can feel your teeth move.

But I hadn't covered all the angles. Just as I bit into the sandwich, the haunting poet uttered this extremely graphic line about an abortion, and I almost lost it. (As you may well know, body references involving flesh and bellies and loins and stuff are really the meat and potatoes of '90s poetry. Readers commonly end a string of carnal nouns with a starkly pensive "and blood...." I don't know what all this blood is about, but it sounds as if the authors don't either, because they invariably end that line with what sounds a lot like a question mark.)

I waited for a safe moment before I ventured the next bite. Bombed again. Right when I'd gotten a big chomp on some rare meat and tomatoes, she started in about sticky blood and some stuff you don't want to hear about, and I almost tossed the sandwich out, but I was so, so hungry. I decided to shake out the tomatoes and maybe that would help. And wait, again, for the right moment. The merciful poet started talking about a circus and I thought, *finally*, and stuffed practically the whole rest of the sandwich in my mouth while I had the chance, but I was immediately hit with the phrase "pink plastic dildo" and I gagged right out loud and had to make use of the fire exit before I gave her something else pink to write about.

When can you say you've really tried? I feel a responsibility to be up on things, to get with the program, but I think it's unanimous that I'm better off left out in the cold this time. Maybe if they had video monitors out in the hall as they do at those fancy theaters, I could get a load of this hip poetry with the pressure off. There could even be some kind of discounted hallway price for people like me who can't sit still. Poetry for the Puerile or something. It would be like instant syndication revenue. Think of it!

I don't know, maybe my future is really in marketing.

That Is to Say...

Yesterday morning I was fishing for compliments regarding a valiant laundry stint. I caught a bullhead, in the form of my husband's amiable acknowledgment, "I know, and don't think it didn't go unappreciated, either."

That afternoon I discovered that my self-coiffed hair had some sort of hapless antenna sticking out of the top of it. My husband tried to reassure me that no one would notice, but I kept wailing that I wanted him to be proud of me. He soothed, "Dear, I couldn't *be* proud of you."

I spent the evening sampling the paint and water for lead content. There had to be an explanation.

And there was. Both of these innocently-delivered insults had come from an unfortunate blending of two clichéd phrases. Once I broke that code, my mind flooded with dozens of similar hybrids I have heard:

My mother-in-law is still trying to teach her son manners. Trying to direct him to refrain from eating until I had reached the dinner table, she admonished discreetly, "Let's not wait 'til Bonny gets here."

That etiquette foible caused her to recall the morning, circa 1940, when she parted ways with her beloved fellow summer campers after a close-knit week. She had spread her arms to embrace the group with a heartfelt "I'm sorry I met you."

My friend once hastened to amend that, even though her father didn't want to travel to her sister's home for Thanksgiving, "it doesn't mean he doesn't love her any less." It's good to know where you stand.

On their fourth day of use, I felt compelled to comment that my husband's boxer shorts were beginning to frighten me. In a join-the-club/you-and-what-army spirit, he exclaimed cheerfully, "Well, join the army!"

At a discount clothing store, the clerk chirped, "And, again, if you have any questions, please don't ask." Discount is as discount goes, I guess.

I overheard someone confidently defining a particular musician's flaw as his "lack of insensitivity to pitch." And they say music today is just noise.

After a harrowing drive home through heavy traffic, my husband complained that I was too slow in closing the car door, getting my keys out, climbing the stairs, and opening the apartment door. I asked him to quit picking on me, and he shot back, "Don't tell me how to boss you around."

On a blustery winter night our friend Gary gallantly opened a door for me. Caught in that allow me/after you trap, he gestured grandly, "After me." As I said, it was blustery. And he's from California.

Sometimes you can't even rely on the excuse of competing phrases:

Recounting what he'd learned from an overview of ancient Greek authors, my husband was filling me in on Sappho. He started to say, "She—"and I interjected that I couldn't believe there was a single "she" in the history of the classics. He enthused, "Oh, yeah! In fact, they say she's the father of—" at which point I was banging my hands on the table, I was laughing so hard. I dimly heard him finish the sentence, "—feminism."

A former boss—and I do mean former—feebly attempted to apply what he was taught at a human resources training retreat: "Now, I don't mean to make anyone feel good here, but the code word for the meeting is communication." There's $5,000 out the window.

Some mistakes are wincingly transparent. Calculating his finances and coming up short, my husband considered whether working overtime at his day job was the best way to bridge the gap. Ultimately, he concluded that he'd do better to get his money another way. But "money" and "another" unfortunately contracted to give birth to the following: "I'm going to get my mother."

Standing in line at the coffee shop early this morning, my husband noticed that this was the day the eleventh punch on his coffee card would allow him a free double latte. He exclaimed, to the groggy confusion of us both and the startlement of the entire coffee line fore and aft, "Hey! I get a free beer!"

My cliché-blending theory is inadequate to capture the guileless wonders of the human tongue. Come to think of it, my husband's tongue is emerging as the prime culprit—I'd better call the lab again to see what's keeping those lead-content tests.

TRUTH IS STRANGER THAN SCIENCE FICTION

It was really only probably a minute and a half.

I was riding down in the elevator from the top floor of a very tall building. A co-worker, in the truest sense, the sense where you just wouldn't claim her with any other title if forced to introduce, entered the elevator with me. Because it's an express car, we had the thing to ourselves for the duration. She is, near as I've ever been able to figure out, a singularly boring and shallow person, well beyond the level to which all workers are necessarily driven.

I noticed something strange right away, in that she was leaning against the back wall uncustomarily close to my habitual cowering post in the back left corner. Uncustomarily close for our Midwest culture, not just for the co-worker. I asked how she was, because I had no choice. She sighed, gazing glassily ahead and slightly skyward. She said, "Oh, I'm okay, it's just this science fiction."

As an old boss was once (and probably still is) fond of shouting, "Whoa, time out." Here was this drone recognizing her condition. Recognizing our condition. The unreality of our surroundings, the fact that we work up in the sky and can open no windows. The relentless, cacophonous, silent whirring of proliferating business machines so close to our ears. Day in and day out.

She said, "Maybe it's the circulation." Yes, the body's blood must pool at our feet as we sit, folded, for grossly unnatural periods of time. And there are those who circulate constantly, asking you, because you're next, how you are in the third person. (So how's Bonny today? they ask me as they park themselves for the immovable twenty minutes they must encompass with this and other unmotivated questions.) Something like neon circulates through the graying fluorescent lights. Fluorine?

She said, still leaning, still staring, "I'm so tired, I can't do anything." That's just it, that's the nature of science fiction. When you are against the wall (and she was), when your soul speaks to you that you're living in a vacuum, when your mind is filled with dully floating particles of paper dust, it is then that you cannot act, although act you must. *Il faut s'agir*, that whole existential thing. It's an impossible conflict, and one of the most common of modern living.

She said, "I think a lot of people around me had it first." Now, that I knew. I just didn't know she knew. There are those who had already acted, who had moved back to Milwaukee, who had sung at a wedding, who had at least tried to boat to Bimini from the tip of Florida but the water was too cold. There are those who had simply been leaning and staring for some time. There is even one on the fence, one who is known to juice loud vegetables in a large-motored juicer in the middle of the office with a blank but ever so slightly mean expression on her face.

She said, leaning deeper into the elevator wall, "Maybe if I got some medication." Well, I wasn't going to say anything, and I hadn't, but clearly medication would be indicated here. On the other hand, if she, this bland-turned-plagued creature, needs medication to quell her awakening, then maybe we all do. Or no one does. Is it moral to mute a budding intolerance, to assimilate the surreal buzz of the everyday from whence came the crisis? But then, how to continue on "as you were, men" once you see just how it was that you were?

So much more to consider, but we had reached the ground floor and the elevator door opened. As is the unspoken rule between co-workers, we promptly diverged with half-masted waves and mumblings about "Have a good lunch" as we brisked off in the opposite direction, opposite meaning an instant assessment of the other's probable compass and a commitment to countering that reading.

It was only as I was spinning through the revolving door to the out-of-doors, her words echoing in my head, "It's just this science fiction, it's just this science fiction," that it all came together. Like an FBI agent replaying a tape segment over and over for a clue, I was rewarded as I propelled out into the crowd, but it didn't feel like a reward:

"It's just this sinus infection."

The Tarmac Is Restricted to the Travel Buff

What's the deal with everybody saying "tarmac" all the time as if the word were as comfy on the tongue as an old shoe?

There seems to be a new trend where certain strange and possibly invented words are suddenly adopted as basic, longstanding vocabulary. I don't think "tarmac" is even on the GRE test, but it's bandied about these days like your best friend's middle name.

It has come to my attention that the tarmac might be a well-established element of airport technology, and not a type of turtle that evolved from the dinosaur, after all. Its use in a sentence either has to do with Bill Clinton jogging or with refugees, near as I can gather so far, and it doesn't appear to be one of those pieces of highway that float at sea and receive planes using a large rubber band. This appears to be a landlubbing creature. I'm picturing a fresh parking lot (probably just because of the "tar" part of the tarmac; I have no instinct for the "mac" segment), a sort of outdoor bituminous lobby for incoming air travelers and/or their waiting welcomers. Who knows.

All I know is that everybody's doing it. Or at least talking about it, like it's some time-tested potluck hot dish and not a completely foreign word the use for which would be very slight, at best, for the average person. The tarmac strikes me as a term to be reserved for the highest levels of government, and even then to be used only in print, in classified documents, not blabbed into the atmosphere willy-nilly as though national security means nothing to them.

Similarly, I am now inundated with the words "travel buff." I was trying to buy nylons to wear in my sister's wedding. She called me from Colorado and told me the best match for my bridesmaid's dress was something called "lobster bisque." I could see her point. Sounded right, good match.

I set forth to secure three pairs of lobster bisque, only to find that they were part of last season's hose (didn't know there were seasons), and they were now replaced by a pink mist, which color was promptly rejected by my marrying sister as too pink. Right she was. She suggested a salmonish/peachish color, and I agreed, although I was having significant trouble finding the same. She threw in efficiently, "You could always go travel buff."

This was the third time in seven hours I'd heard that confounding characterization in reference to hosiery. Something was definitely up. I found myself wondering whether this faceless fabric was suitable—or even required—attire for the tarmac. I had to know.

This plentiful travel buff, it turns out, asserts itself as some sort of unnerving chameleon creation, at once no color and all colors, hence the fascination. It purports to obviate the need for the elusive lobster bisque, and certainly can take on any relative of the salmon and win.

Still, I would not be sidetracked into some unchristened tunnel.

An unknown consumer at the eighth store (hey, the title Matron of Honor is not to be taken lightly, nor the duties thereto applied) overheard my plea for remaindered lobster bisque and mused aloud that I "could always go travel buff." I pressed on. I'm of the mind that if you've never heard of it you don't need it (although, deep in the night, I yearn desperately for the tarmac—just one look, just one touch).

The clerk at the twelfth store, after conferring rather toll-free with a retail affiliate, abandoned my request for seafaring nylons in favor of a similar observation: travel buff. The phrase had now officially crossed several state borders, a significant fact indeed.

The bottom line is this. I'm sure these words, these secret government fashion words, have a very good reason for existing. Nevertheless, that's no excuse for tossing them about like some sort of Canadian football.

10. ILLOGICAL LOGICAL PHILOSOPHIES

ALL BALLED UP

What if I, being female, were to comment, "That really breaks my balls"? All the gangster movies use that phrase over and over. They're all men. But what if I said that in, say, an office setting? I don't have any of what I claim is breaking, so am I offending anyone? Because if I did have them, surely I would be inviting reprimand. Do I have a leg to stand on pointing out that there's nothing to break in my situation? I think it's actually "busts my balls," if that makes any difference. Or would it be a greater error to reassure another female, "I'm just bustin' your balls," for instance? Am I insulting her by insinuating she has them, or does not? Or is it just the region of their supposed residence that is the objectionable reference and none of these details matters?

What if a large man said it to a small woman? Is that a perceived threat due to likely strength differential, or is it utterly harmless based on the reasonably certain assumption that she lacks the threatened objects? What if she said it to him, and maybe couldn't but would like to carry out the threat, except that the word "break" or "bust" suddenly seems ill-chosen and she gets distracted from her goal, trying to think of a more appropriate action verb?

Oh, I have so many questions. If I marketed a brand of cigarettes called "Surgeon General," would that be illegal? Could I be court-martialed? Why does anyone ever go to Radio Shack? We vow, "Never again." Yet we return.

Do you think for one second that the major car company using the melody of an old Shaker verse ("'Tis a gift to be simple, 'tis a gift to be free…") is paying the Shaker community royalties? Would they accept royalties while objecting to the excesses of money and the luxury car itself?

How would the money be divided? What if the Shakers got all in an uproar over fair compensation between members, whether the elders get more or less than the new mothers? What if they spent all their resources suing to stop the car company from using the melody because the car isn't simple, but then the community has nothing left but simplicity. What of check number inflation? They won't accept checks under 1000, or 3000, or whatever the number, but even those fake checks you get from the credit card companies start with 500, and many times you can request the number you want the checks to start with at a new account.

I want a check that starts with 0001 and counts up from there. There's no chance for those checks where you have to write your own address in the corner. And what about the idea that a check is just a promise, can be written on paper, in any form, really? What about that episode of *Love, American Style* where the guy wrote a huge check on the girl's bikini'd stomach in rare berry juice, and the bank had only to run a test on the berry juice to ascertain that it was indeed from a deserted island and therefore good and cashable? And what's to prevent her from cashing it at juice labs all over the country, the world? Would it be a transgression for a bank to cancel the check on her body in permanent ink? Would it be on her back or, improperly, across the front? What if it were canceled on her back and another bank, with a front-cancel in mind, didn't ask her to turn around? Could she be held accountable? Probably. She's all balled up.

CLEAR AND PRESENT DANGER

I am going through the Age of Fear, and frankly I've picked a bad time. Just when I decide that every move I make is a near-death experience, that I could choke to death on every bite of food, that every gas oven is about to explode, every little pain is a heart attack, and every stranger has an itchy trigger finger, I am presented with an unprecedented string of objectively terrifying events.

My husband and I had just embarked on a road trip, a vacation from the Age of Fear. But the interstate hotel we stayed at the first night had planted letterhead correspondence all over the room—on the pillows, on the table next to the two mints, on the TV, on the door next to the three bolts—telling us 16 things we could do to minimize the threat of bodily harm being done to us during our stay, although it was clear that our efforts would be futile. Actually, I think that was Number 16, but I can't be sure because my husband swiftly confiscated all the correspondence.

We snuck out of there bright and early, past snacking seniors and splashing children. We escaped to Leadville, to the highest altitude hotel in the entire U.S., to get away from it all. So we checked into this idyllic bed-and-breakfast and began our climb to the third floor, which felt suspiciously like a climb up the mountains that towered outside our window. While my husband promptly chose to lie down on the floor of our room, I, ever vigilant, searched for possible instructions or warnings. I was rewarded with a framed decree stating that we would experience numerous unpleasant and terrifying symptoms due to our altitude. It was recommended that we lie with our feet over our heads and, as you can imagine, by the time we were found and revived and told that that didn't mean a perpetual headstand, it was almost checkout time.

We headed for the plains. Trying to learn from our mistakes, we chose a flat motel in a flat town in rural Kansas. Who knew that The Weather Channel found it convenient to report Kansas tornadoes in the unit of "dozens"? The one time that my husband was able to snap me out of my tornadic Age of Fear panic trance (I think we were on Tornado 26 out of 48), he convinced me that I might be effectively distracted from our inevitable doom by some video games in the lobby. (There was no basement. Yes, they were sure of that, because I asked if perhaps they had overlooked the basement in past years. No, they hadn't.)

There was available only one pinball game: Whirlwind. You hear a recording say, "A storm is coming! Head for the cellar!" while a fan at the top of the pinball machine starts whirring and you see a picture at the back of the machine of a big whirlwind with a sign hanging by one nail: "Welcome to Kansas." As a result of my fervor to get the pinball into the "cellar" (at least it had a cellar), the machine was taken ill, displaying such symptoms as a nervous and random flapping of all of the flippers and bumpers in a spasmic rattle, then quiet, then the rattling again. I finally had to get the manager out from under the desk to fix the machine.

Riding on the tail of Tornado 48, we scurried for home, through lightning and flash floods, effectively straddling one headlight-dazed possum near Ottumwa, Iowa. Repeating softly that there's no place like home, we finally pulled into our sunny neighborhood only to hear a whirring sound. Looking up, we spotted an FBI helicopter circling tirelessly over our heads. Well, it was bound to happen. I was finally going to be caught in a traditional Age of Fear crossfire.

I did enjoy a brief respite from the Tour of Fear. Flipping my way to The Weather Channel, I happened upon a show consisting solely of apparent blooper outtakes of the Dalai Lama laughing and laughing, laughing and laughing.

THIS MAY COME AS A SHOCK...

I woke up from my nap in a slow panic the other day. Creeping (sort of literally) toward 50 years old, I realized my life was irrevocably almost 50 percent over. Wiping the sleep from my doomed eyes, I recognized naps for what they are: slow suicide. Let's face it. I've been taking a long walk on a short pier.

It finally hit me that I am bound for certain death. No matter what. Even if I live to be 100 (which is entirely possible, if Grandma's any indication), that is a finite number. I took math. Don't try to confuse me.

So I sat up on the couch in the bleak light of mid-afternoon to face the truth. I'm a runaway train. Headed for disaster. No matter what I do, I'll end up in the same unenviable condition. Dead as a doornail. I don't even know what a doornail is, and even if I did, I'd be just as obliterated with that one additional fact stuffed into my head as without it.

There I was, huddled forlornly amidst the pillows, picking loose threads off my slippers, when "The Eve of Destruction" came on the radio.

The not-so-eternal optimist, I soon saw the bright side. Knowing you're done for isn't all bad because it logically eliminates the usefulness of phobias. For instance, the fear of flying. I can now freely shed my terror of airplanes, because what I really was worried about was a plane crash, right? And what do those result in? Exactly.

Well, as it turns out, even if not one single plane disintegrates with me strapped inside it, my goose is still cooked. My lurking omens and my adamant refusal to board any plane smaller than a 747 and my lucky turtle earrings were all crafty plans to deny the persistent fact that my rocket is poised for the sky.

So of course I shuffled off the couch and called my travel agent. I'm heading straight to Europe for two reasons.

First, obviously, I wasn't fooling streetwise Mother Nature by avoiding air travel. And second, when I get back I'll be eight hours younger than when I leave Europe. This way I'm killing two birds with one stone, but it's no big deal because they would have croaked anyway.

CANADIAN ROCKIES: THOSE AREN'T ROCKS!

Like anybody, I'm always exhilarated when spring has sprung, but I'd prefer that it not spring at me from the alpine trees in the pitch black night.

Here in Banff National Park, where I've boldly scheduled my first communion with Mother Nature, there's more than one kind of mountain. Sure, there are the Rockies, but there are also these other very, very large structures that look like white boulders until your eyes get accustomed to the terrain and you realize these boulders have legs. I'm told that they are elk, and very pregnant elk at that. Local legend has it that things can get ugly during the incipient stages of mother-elkhood. Their heavy-gazed plodding turns to purposeful and lightning-fast charging toward the curious.

When I first arrived in Banff, I was assured that the fabled calving season wouldn't occur for a couple of months. Once I'd paid for my three-week stay and hung up my clothes, the news was leaked to me that calving could begin in a couple of weeks. I went straight to a phone and staged an urgent interview with a corollary adventurer in Colorado: "Have you seen an elk? What do you do?" He had just recently seen one appear on the wrong side of a protective fence. It, that mammoth rock, leapt over the six-foot barrier without effort. I pressed, "So, what did you do?" He replied sagely, "I just kept the car moving."

Some help.

Fortunately, the first close-range sighting I weathered was by car, when two elk with huge, broken antlers and scraps of fur missing picked their way, as if teetering on high heels, across the busy main road of Banff. While I gaped at this apparent insurrection, cabs swerved in annoyance, and pedestrians didn't so much as turn their heads. One woman was walking down the sidewalk, led by two tiny dogs on a leash. I twisted around in the driver's seat and caught her eye, gesturing toward the elk and turning up my palms, the international sign for "If that don't beat all!" Her eyes danced with merriment, at my expense, as her two shrubby critters advanced blithely toward the reigning powers of the town.

I waited up for the sauntering elk and followed them at trolling speed. It soon became clear that these dainty giants were going to church. They crossed the lawn to the doors of the chapel, and I just missed their polite nod to the pastor in the sunny doorway because a taxi was honking behind me.

I've always been chided that it's silly to worry about bears, because I'll only see black bears around this time of year; the grizzlies don't come around for a couple more months. Yeah, right. That's what they said about calving season. I'm not falling for that old line again. "And besides," the natives said, "just don't surprise the bear. They hate to be surprised." Oh, and I don't? "Let them know you're there, then look them in the nose—not the eyes—and back away, taking care to stay facing the bear all the while." Until you're skewered in the back by an elk?

I went into a mountain store, the kind that have ice cleats and stuff, and saw a basket of bear bells at the register. I told the mountaineer at the counter that I understood the part about how the bells would keep me apprised of the bear's whereabouts, but I didn't understand (1) how to get the bell necklace over the bear's head and (2) what to do if there's yet another bear I don't know about and therefore haven't greeted Hawaiian style. The jolly pandemonium among the clerks gave me the feeling I've got it all wrong somehow.

Suddenly I remembered something that made all this fretting seem foolish. I recalled a personal safety workshop I attended once that told you how to protect yourself and take control. So, if I see a bear, all I need to do is point boldly at it (at its nose, in this case, I guess) and announce forcefully, "NO. STAY WHERE YOU ARE. I'M WALKING ALONE." The instructor had said that the troublemaker usually prefers an easy target and would not want to stick around and struggle with me.

On the way back to the hotel, I almost ran over a white fox, which actually froze in the headlights, and I braced myself for the caribou/coyotes lurking among the mountain trees. I'm not sure they're the same animal—I think one's bigger—but I know they're around somewhere because every store in town is named one or the other.

The minute I'd locked the door to my room safely behind

me, I made the wilderness survival decision to start the next morning with a trip to the hot springs in order to begin untangling my elkbound muscles.

Bright and early, hoping the animals were still sleeping off their terroristic capers of the night before, I followed the hot springs signs up a winding hill. Pretty soon I came upon an iron gate and turned in. There was a little stone structure with what looked to be a well in the middle. This had to be the place.

I was really looking forward to finally jumping into the steaming sulfur. I'd had to pass up the opportunity in Thermopolis, Wyoming once due to too much beer-and-corncob stew around the campfire. Now I would make up for that. The hot springs would renew my strength and make me immortal so the elk can't hurt me. Or am I thinking of the Fountain of Youth? Maybe the sulfur spring just imbues one with an odor repulsive to animals.

Anyway, I bounded toward the well, crowing, "Last one in is a–" and I was midleap when I saw the rustic wooden sign: "Bat Sanctuary."

How could I be so wrong?

I pled with the bats to let me find my own way home, babbling that I really didn't—thanks, though—need a lift.

By the time I'd teased the fiendish winged rodents out of my hair and scrambled back to the car, I had a new perspective on large mammals.

At this point, I'm saying, I don't even care if the elk do lay their eggs before I get out of the park; protective mothers can't be worse than sanctified bats.

UP WITH THE SUNSET

What is this thing that I like to call The Midwest Hostility about getting up late?

When I was in junior high and we would go to the Farmer's Market, downtown under the bridge, my parents would dare me to ask the farmers how early they got up. There would only be a few of them still around when we got there, and only a few turnips and such still available to buy. I would bite and say to a guy, Okay, when did you get up this morning? And he'd say 4 a.m. And my parents would smile and say, See? And I never did see.

I can't picture those farmers dealing out poker at 3 a.m. or catching David Letterman (even the new time slot). And I don't get this feeling in New York. It's a sun-based thing. Up with the sun, down with the sun, because you can't light a field. But I don't work a field; I have never worked a field. I type. Why do I need to follow a farming schedule?

Last night I went to bed at 2 a.m. (Okay, 3 a.m. See, it's like dieting, you always want to cheat a little if interrogated.) I drank too much coffee after midnight and got too hyped up speculating on all kinds of gossip and then, to lull myself to sleep, I read some more of *Presumed Innocent* and found out that the prosecuting attorney was being charged with the murder he was investigating (which I should have known, because that was the whole point of the movie, the late show of which I went to twice).

Like I'm really going to be able to sleep now.

But I tried to, and almost succeeded, and then the heavy

metal music started up, as it tends to, at 4:30 a.m. one apartment up and one over. Blaring, intolerable. This goes on for an hour and a half and I am too tired to go up and make it stop. So as the robins start chirping I close all the windows and unplug the phone and settle in for the night as the sun comes up.

It is a quarter to two in the afternoon when I wake up. And 2:30 by the time I've taken my bath and made the canned cinnamon rolls and fielded the crabby calls that came in the split instant the phone was reconnected and gotten my mitts around a cup of coffee (hair of the dog what bit me). And all I feel is guilt. Not about these irretrievable hours of my life, but about how I've let the farmers down. Again.

Now the next several hours will be wasted worrying about how the sun is on a downward slide, and I'll be forced to stay up as late as I can to balance things out, which will take a lot of coffee, and on it goes.

I'm a fish out of bed living in the Heartland.

How Sweet It Is

Several years ago, I bought my niece a book from the *Sweet Valley High* pre-teen series for Christmas. I was sitting on my bed on Christmas Eve, about to wrap this little pink book. I flipped it over to position it on the wrapping paper. A large-lettered teaser asked whether a terrible secret would be discovered in time. I had to know. I opened to the middle and instantly got caught up in the story. I started from the beginning so as not to miss a word, and stayed up until four in the morning to finish the book.

I straggled in to the Christmas morning festivities a Sweet Valley junkie. I had to have more. For a good several months, I read at least one a week and loved every word. Then I had to give it up.

For a very feeble and powerful reason. That's right, embarrassment. Because high-powered professionals would catch me reading those great little books at lunch and I'd turn bright red and tell them I just finished *Let Us Now Praise Famous Men* and they didn't look convinced. Because my friend wouldn't let her thirteen-year-old daughter read them because they were beneath her reading level.

Let's face it. I was shamed out of one of my favorite luxuries. I moved from buying them at Borders to buying them at Woolworth's, where nobody cares and where they staple it inside a bag. After enough chastisement (and even mere sidelong glances), I stopped buying them altogether. They were getting me depressed. I'd sit in the tub reading a bath-length book about Elizabeth and Jessica Wakefield at the school dance, and I'd be saying, *maybe everyone's right, I should be running for Congress or something instead.*

Tell me, though, why do people think it's funny if men play video games, and even impressive if women do, and it's deadly serious that we watch men kicking or throwing or hitting balls on TV, but I can't read about Sweet Valley High? It must be that literary thing, where you can have your mindless fun, sure, but not while you're reading, as if that act were sacred. What about reading Ann Landers' column or the funny papers? People are forever asking if I saw the latest "Dilbert" cartoon. They even cut them out and put them on the fridge.

So maybe it's the number of words. Maybe it's okay for a page or two, but not 134 pages. Or there's some theory that if you read the *Sweet Valley High* books you're ruined for any other literature. People always seem to think that's all I read. But wait, I'm trying not to give in to that judgment thing. Even if I read one a day and read nothing else, so what? Why is it that you can collect Coke cans, play hockey, play pinball, even suntan, for heaven's sake, with everyone's blessing, although none of these requires a high IQ, but you can't let unchallenging recreation seep into the printed word category?

That does it. I'm going right out to by *Sweet Valley High* #13 superthriller, *Double Trouble*. And while we're at it, you may as well know that I'm a huge Barry Manilow fan and I never miss a monster truck derby. There. I feel a lot better now.

11. BONNY
GODDESS COW WOMAN

CRACKING THE BIG GOOSE EGG

I have always been bad at sports. Bad at skiing, bad at tennis, bad at swimming, bad at bicycling, bad at basketball, bad at fishing, bad at weightlifting, bad at racquetball, bad at running, bad at baseball, bad at rollerblading, bad at golf, bad at hockey, bad, bad, bad. No matter what sport I'm into, someone's got to tell me what to do every second. Hustle, back up, move forward, run, run, run. I must be pretty bad to need that much help.

Lately, though, I've noticed that my helpers have something in common. They can barely trouble themselves to pass, throw, serve, or otherwise return the ball in question. They wait until the bouncing subsides and it rolls gently to their feet. All the while they're telling me to run up to the ball, get with it, get under it, get moving, don't just stand there. I'm sweating like a pig (actually, pigs don't sweat) and they appear to be practicing meditation.

How did this happen? How did everyone else become my teacher? As I puzzled over this phenomenon, all these exceptions to "everyone" kept stealing over my brain: Sally wouldn't do that, and she's great at tennis. Janet wouldn't do that, and she's great at basketball. Then I realized the obvious answer. "Everyone" is men. Let's face it, men appear to have an open invitation to give sports advice.

Even when they're no good.

Here I am, blissfully hitting tennis balls one day, and a total stranger in a fishing hat marches right into my court and plants his feet not two yards from me, arms folded, in that standing-there way of a know-it-all. He sighs hyper-patiently and asks if I want to know what I'm doing wrong. Suddenly, something like disgust comes over me and I hear myself saying that no, strangely enough, I don't. He starts in anyway, with the requisite unflagging smugness, "Don't you even want to know the most basic things you're doing wrong?

I shut him down. He didn't get to bark one single command. Because I decided, then and there, to invoke a strict no-advice policy, effective immediately. I told him I came here to play alone, in privacy, without interruption.

You can imagine the ensuing spewing. How can I expect to get any better, to finally reach his level of mediocrity, if I'm so darn stubborn I won't listen to reason?

I'll tell you how. Peace and quiet. When I can hear myself think, I feel myself play. Believe it or not, I can tell when I'm doing it right. And suddenly I'm rocketing to competence. Across the veritable smorgasbord of sports. I'm sinking baskets, I'm slamming tennis balls, I'm one over par, I'm hooking fighting fish. Stand back, I'm on a roll.

Strangely enough, men are no longer eager to compete with me. (Scare me some more, right?) Either they're nonplussed at being relegated to that uneasy status of equal, or they're just afraid of a little sweat.

I, for what it's worth, boys, once earned that Presidential Fitness thing and got a medal in the long jump before I was old enough to understand that I was a hopeless case.

NO, PLEASE, AFTER YOU, AND YOU, AND YOU...

I have long maintained that I am not a victim of subservient socialization. Nobody walks over me. Because I stand up for myself in an unseemly fashion, believe you me.

Take today, for instance. Not ten minutes ago, a man spit in my face. But he didn't mean it. So it doesn't count. See, intentions go a long, long way in my book. End results are essentially immaterial to my value system. Not that I don't treat each case individually. I assessed the situation as I dried my face.

The way I see it, the poor guy got on the bus, took the window seat in front of me, slid open the window, and spat out into the wind, which propelled his spit in an arc and deposited it on my face, directly under my nose. Without turning around, the guy sang out, "Excuse me!" as I wiped the gluey gob off my upper lip, thinking, boy, this really burns me up.

But he did excuse himself, this Richard-Dreyfus-meets-Alan-Alda guy with a tense beard and a denim belt with embroidered flowers on it, and that's all you can ask. And it isn't as though he faced me squarely and spat in my eye. If I've ever had a close call, though, in terms of testing my know-my-rights mettle, this was it. It was hard to remind myself he had said those two magic words because I kept getting distracted by his breath, which was the scratch'n'sniff souvenir he had left on my upper lip. As I said, that was close.

And then, as luck would have it, I was repeatedly punched about the face that self-same day. There I was at a lecture, the subject of which I never did catch because the guy two seats down had this chronic I-like-to-take-up-space-because-I've-got-a-disproportionately-large-or-small-ego habit of stretching his arms straight out from his sides, fists clenched, and consequently his right fist came within an air puff of my left cheek approximately every 75 seconds.

If he had been in my way, things would've gotten ugly. But fortunately I wasn't using the space to the very immediate left of my left cheek, so no harm done. If I'd had to, say, whisk away a gnat from my left eye, though, there would have been hell to pay. Although there's no reason I couldn't whisk quickly, between punches, with my right hand.

In my book, rational thought and creative problem-solving can avert all manner of needless confrontation. Punching, spitting, whatever, it's all just part of the fabric of life. I say you can rebel against every little thing or you can see these human events as natural, beautiful. No reason to get all in a huff.

I don't, strictly speaking, need my space.

WHATEVER HAPPENED TO JANE RUSSELL GUSHING, "HURRY, FULL-FIGURED GALS!"?

I've about had it with this mad scientist angle they're using on women's "health and beauty" advertising. It seems to me that women's product advertisers are pulling some kind of vocabulary caper that we're supposed to react to with awe and obedience.

It's time we admit that no woman knows or cares what all these bogus laboratory terms really mean, and that propeller-beanied ad men are banking on our meek ignorance. But their ploy, if you think about it, ends up backfiring every time. Try a little quick-draw word association on these scam tech phrases, and health and beauty don't look so attractive:

Makeup (now, there's a noun for you) at the fancy department store counters is now labeled "non-comedogenic." So help me, all I can come up with is that people will stop laughing at my face if I use the stuff. I think there's some caveat in there about how I have to spend over $85.00 to ensure its success.

Deodorant, we are reassured, is now "pH balanced for women." I'm guessing that means it won't tip over when you set it down. (That is reassuring, because I have enough tipping-over worries whenever I look at the international symbol for women on the public bathroom doors. The woman's two legs come out of the skirt fused into one sharp point that would give way to even a half-hearted tug on gravity's part.)

Earrings are all hypoallergenic these days. Don't you think recycling has gone too far if the posts for pierced earrings are now made from broken pieces of infected needles? I mean, it's only a planet. Get a grip.

The chic-est yogurts proclaim that they contain "active cultures." I don't know, but it would seem to me like sound marketing to keep your salmonella problems under wraps. That kind of disclosure is better reserved for the point when push comes to shove in the class action lawsuit. The 21st Century is no time for earnestness and coming clean.

Even such a staple as hand lotion is enhanced with lanolin. I'm assuming that's some sort of Swedish grease imported at my considerable expense. That's how they keep everything so darned tidy over there—patch off all the grease to the additive-romanced capitalists. No by-products wasted, you know, that whole Swedish efficiency thing. Hogs, Americans, whatever. There's always a taker out there.

The ad trend is to throw in some enticing technical terms to get credit for a nod toward women's intelligence while taking full advantage of our fear of admitting we don't understand something. So no matter what they say we just hear, "Take my word for it. You wouldn't understand, but this thing is good for you." And we accept that, because stuff with extra words on it costs more, and higher prices are comforting.

Don't get me wrong, I look for stuff that has those big words on it. I seek it out. Because, like all serious consumers, I want to look healthy and beautiful. But what do I know. These ads could say just about anything and I'd still go around requesting the latest chemical miracle of the white-coated cosmetic clerk, if she doesn't get to me first, with possibly neither one of us having a clue what the hell is going on.

Here are a few educated guesses I've made, based on the exciting advances in science today, on product claims that will soon be seen in finer stores everywhere:

- With squichelle star-gazing capabilities
- Comes with a uniform-based reactive code
- Packed with caramelized opportunity crystals
- Notice the new satchel-confounding spittoon feature
- Camel-backed and wheater than ever!
- !!NOW!! Squared-off with adverse rotundity!

See? We're just a bunch of high-class garbage goats (no offense to goats, who don't actually eat tin cans but enjoy a good paperback).

Don't even get me started on wear-dated carpet, or I'll hit the acoustic ceiling.

I'M RATTLING MY OWN CAGE NOW

When I first tried on hockey skates, late last winter, sitting on the unheated second floor of the hardware store, I worried that they looked too tough. They were black and worn out and nothing like the crisp white figure skates with the powder blue foam lining that I kept so clean. But when I wrapped that bright yellow tape around the stick (I still have no idea why you're supposed to do that), I started to itch for the ice, which was melting rapidly.

So this year I couldn't wait to get out there. I was still traveling at less than two miles per hour on skates, but I had learned to pull the laces tighter than I could stand, and that helped with the wobble. I was learning to stop hockey-style, although in pointlessly slow motion. But practice helped, and just last week I finally got the puck to lift off the ground, which is a moment to celebrate. My husband tells me that when he was little, when boys played hockey and girls missed out big time, the burning question was, "Can you lift?" So now he asks me that all the time just so I can say, "Yeah, can you?"

In between all these practices I've been right out there on the ice, playing goalie in the neighborhood game. No one has made a motion to throw me off the team or so much as commented about what's a girl doing in the cage. And believe me, I've been waiting, all the while acting ever so casual, like it's no big deal, like I belong there. And I'm just bursting with this big secret as I go about my day: Hey, I'm a goalie! You just sold a pen refill to a goalie!

Last week my husband took me to the sporting goods store and pelted pucks at me while I tried on different goalie pads (stick with those old metal-plated ones!), and nobody even laughed. I think people kind of wished we'd get the heck out of the aisle so they could get past, but that was about the extent of it. My pride at being blasé about the whole thing was giving way to a sort of hurt bewilderment, kind of like it was my birthday and nobody would admit it.

What did I expect? After all, the Penguins have a female goalie on second string, and I hear there's an expansion team with a first-string female goalie. Not to mention that half the Mighty Ducks lineup was girls, which was not even an issue in the plot!

I think it took a puck to the head to make me see that this is it. This is it. All I ever wanted was the chance to do what men do without a commotion, and here it is. *Hockey.*

BECAUSE I'M BIGGER THAN YOU, THAT'S WHY

A curious and not altogether pleasant phenomenon has happened to me. Through no intention of my own, I have lost somewhere heading toward 15 pounds in the last couple weeks. I decided it's time to cut out salt (I've had this Old Dutch thing going on that had to stop), and it turns out salt is jealously attached to fat. So I keep finding myself either eating something ridiculously tastelessly healthy, which is hardly tempting me to reach for thirds, or not eating at all because there's usually nothing on entire menus that isn't preserved for all eternity. I'm beginning to resent the percentage of the price of a sandwich that represents refrigerating the meat. You talk about playing fast and loose with our precious energy resources.

So now my clothes are all but falling off, and I find myself holding in my stomach while leaning over to brush my teeth, only to find that it isn't necessary because it isn't even hanging out. And long t-shirts have started hanging like a sheet instead of bunching up about the jeans pockets. God, how I've envied people whose t-shirts fall like a sheet. Now I've got so much energy I even feel more like exercising, and maybe someday I will. I scurry around washing dishes and sorting mail and cutting my toenails. Okay, okay, we all get the idea.

Except one thing. I'm not sure I like it.

I take up less space. In my clothes, in the world. I am less substantial. I grab at myself and can't get hold of a handful of what I once thought was a medical condition on or about the stomach which my doctor blandly pronounced "just subcutaneous fat."

I read this article by Roseanne Barr once where she said her advice to anyone was to be as big as you can. And I took that to mean every which way. Loud, strong, and just plain big. But I look at myself now, all lean and accepted at most major department stores and a sure bet to be sacrificed to the middle seat of the car whenever it's called for, and I can just see old gray doctors checking those bogus '50s weight charts they schemed up and nodding sinister approval, and frankly it's giving me the creeps.

Months back, at this year's State Fair, I went to four grandstand concerts, a record even for me. The first three concerts drew fashion plate crowds. I always wore the same black sweatshirt and jeans and generally faded into the darkening sky while I scanned the fashion plate (what do they mean by "plate," anyway?) set with a sort of alienated and shiftless desire to look like them.

But then came Concert #4, the blues concert. I had just

begun my trudge up the familiar grandstand steps in my concert-going uniform when a sensation flowed over me that went something like: aaahhh, home at last. I looked around and saw only the kindred spirits of strangers. I spotted this woman crossing over to the next section, and I elbowed my husband and said, Look, quick! That's what I want to look like at her age. She's my idol.

He followed my jabbing finger to this self-announcing woman of maybe sixty, stuffed into her blue jeans and barging peacefully ahead in a nondescript tan concert t-shirt and an old suede jacket. She had long earrings and big round rose-colored glasses and strong brown hair that wrestled its way down her back—and she was beefy.

And I thought, oh, yeah, that's where I'm headed. Because she had both boots on the ground and she took up space and she just *was*. I took stock of myself as she ranged into the crowd and thought, well, I'm not beefy yet, but I'm not slight either. Give me time.

About the Author

Bonny Belgum divides her time between Minnesota and Wisconsin. That is, she sleeps in Minnesota and buys groceries in Wisconsin. Once upon a time, she eked out a bachelor's degree in psychology at the University of Minnesota, home of behaviorism. Bonny will salivate at the sound of a Blackberry alarm even if she doesn't get the Xanax. She is unjustifiably proud of her pigs, goats, chickens, sheep, and barn cats, all of whom pretty much fend for themselves. She is justifiably proud of her Newfoundland, Sonny, and her husband, Erik, because she changes their water and picks up their socks. Bonny is also a lifelong writer of what she now understands are humorous essays. She used to call them plain old notebooks from age 11 to age 27, when she learned they could garner 50 bucks, albeit on a highly intermittent reward schedule—the most addictive kind. Bonny's stuff has shown up in the likes of the *Atlanta Journal-Constitution*, the *St. Paul Pioneer Press*, and the *Minneapolis Star Tribune*. And some other places too esoteric to mention. Before that, she had a five-year gig as the regular humor columnist for *The Minnesota Women's Press*, a place that understands sometimes all you can do is laugh. A highly social hermit (a term-in-progress), Bonny prefers to stay home if at all possible to avoid the aftermath of human contact. However, with the country going to hell in a handbasket, she has overcome her crippling fear of flying enough to sort of master a Cessna 152 and can point it roughly northward. If it all comes down, Canada's not that far from here.

1748078

Made in the USA